QUESTIONS
20
GOD
wants to ask
YOU

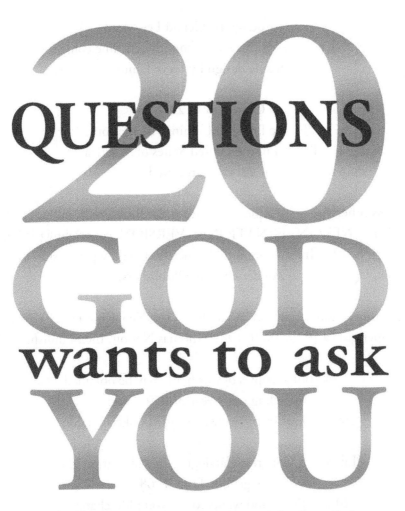

20 QUESTIONS GOD wants to ask YOU

Life-changing encounters with the divine

TROY FITZGERALD

Pacific Press®
Publishing Association
Nampa, Idaho | www.pacificpress.com

Cover design by Gerald Lee Monks
Cover design resources from dreamstime.com
Inside design by Steve Lanto

Copyright © 2008 by
Pacific Press® Publishing Association
Printed in the United States of America

Additional copies of this book may be obtained
by calling toll-free 1-800-765-6955
or online at http://www.adventistbookcenter.com

Library of Congress Cataloging-in-Publication Data
Fitzgerald, Troy, 1968-
20 questions God wants to ask you : life-changing
encournters with the Divine / by Troy Fitzgerald.
p. cm.
ISBN 978-0-8163-2275-6 (paperback)
1. Christian life—Seventh-day Adventist authors. 2. Christian life—
Biblical teaching. 3. Bible—Criticism, interpretation, etc.
I. Title: twenty questions God wants to ask you. II. Title.
BV4501.3.F577 2008
248.4—dc22
2008001445

March 2022

Dedication

This book is dedicated to Cameron, my first born male child. Your love for God is so real, and I'm always amazed by the way you respond to God's voice in your life. You are an inspiration to me, and while I'll always be your dad, I'm honored to have you as my friend. May your answers to God's questions always lead you to deeper love and enduring faithfulness.

Contents

Introduction

The goal of the game *20 Questions* is to discover the identity of an object by asking questions that prompt a "Yes" or "No" answer. Each answer, by process of identification and elimination, functions as a clue as to what the object may be. Fortunately, the rules state the players must deduce the identity of the object in no more than twenty questions. (I'm glad it's *20 Questions* and not *50 Questions*.)

I think the game is annoying. There is something refreshing and efficient about a straight answer. No guessing games, no innuendos—only direct and clear communication minus the spin and nuances. I'm not interested in patching all the complicated pieces together just in order to get a simple answer. The only redeeming quality of the game is that the players are forced to formulate thoughtful questions in order to gain the most information.

In this book, in contrast, it is God who will ask you the questions. And it's not a game; in fact, answering these questions can transform your life.

Questions are what I call the *power tools* of human communication. Questions are loaded with power that prompt people into all sorts of reactions:

Questions provoke: "Oh yeah, what are you going to do about it?" asks the bully on the playground.

Questions invite: "Would you like to go out this Saturday night?" begs the young man to the young lady.

Questions investigate: "Where were you at eleven at night on July twenty-seven, 2005?" the police officer inquires of the suspect.

Questions undermine: "Is it true that she doesn't have any experience in management?" the jealous coworker asks in the break room.

Questions examine: "Why do you want to change your major?" the wise mother inquires of a confused daughter.

One powerful attribute of questions is that they often convey a message rather than collect information. For example, when my father would warn me about my bad behavior, he would ask, "Troy, do you want a spanking?" What kind of question is that? It's true that warnings often come camouflaged in the skin of a question because a question is a more effective method for getting a response.

Perhaps the greatest value of a question is that it seeks the truth. Inquiry is one of the most active parts of language and possibly the most powerful component of human communication. Doctors question patients; lawyers question witnesses; children question teachers; parents question teenagers. Life is peppered with searching for what is real, genuine, and true. And no one has been questioned more than God.

For centuries, humans have wondered, out loud, the curious thoughts that clutter their minds. I'm one of them. It's only natural that, when you don't have all the information, you ask questions. A tragic death of a small child hammered my community, leaving people painfully confused and angry at God. At the end of the funeral a church member said to me, "I have some questions for God about this one, pastor." I did too. Disaster is almost impossible for me to explain, but what about God? Why doesn't God answer the questions of humanity directly? No guessing games. No *20 Questions*. Straight answers for those who want to know.

Unfortunately, God is not going to personally come down and take the witness stand or show up to the press box for a media event. I believe there may be something more important to God than answering our questions.

Consider the questions that God asks us. What does God want to know? What straight answer does God seek from us? More important than our questions for God might be His questions for us. Maybe the secret to a deeper walk with God lies in our response to the questions God asks.

There are hundreds of such questions recorded in Scripture. God's questions challenge the mind and expose the will. When God inquires, you can be sure that an honest answer is what God wants and maybe just what you need.

The questions God asks become watershed events where the answer you give can become a transforming moment in your journey. Adam and Eve. Moses. Elijah. The disciples. Mary. Examine the scenarios where God asks a question and discover a continental divide between life and death, hope and despair, as well as growth and failure—a watershed response from one side of life to the other. The questions God asks are life's heart-changing, mind-altering inquiries.

I discovered another interesting facet about the power of God's questions. In every scenario in Scripture, the questions God asks people reveal what is important to Him. In a way, God's queries reveal a glimpse of His character. You can learn a lot about a person simply by examining the types of questions they ask. The questions God asks are windows to His heart and doorways to His plan for our lives.

Consider a few moments when God popped a question and see if you can discover something about Him, as well as something about yourself:

"Where are you?" God wants to know if you know how far away you are from Him.

"Where are your accusers?" God wants you to answer out loud so you can hear the timeless truth of grace from your own lips.

"Who do you think I am?" The future of the Christian movement leans fully on your answer.

"Why are you so afraid?" Jesus invites you to name one thing that is bigger than His promise and provision for your future.

"Why are you laughing?" God wants to know what is so funny about His plan for your life.

"Do you believe this?" The Savior questions you at death's door as to the sturdiness of your belief in the resurrection.

"Who are you looking for?" Christ reminds you to be deliberate about the focus of your life.

"Do you know what I have done to you?" God quizzes you on His chief lesson on service.

"What is in your hand?" God wonders if you have room in your life for Him to do extraordinary things with your ordinary daily routine.

Listen to the questions God asks, and then answer Him. Respond openly and honestly. You might be tempted to wait until your answer seems right or more appropriate. Think, reflect, and examine your heart—but, please, respond. Elijah pleaded with the disoriented people of God asking, " 'How long will you waver between two opinions? If the LORD is God, follow him; but if Baal is God, follow him' " (1 Kings 18:21). Elijah is awfully direct. His question exposes their problem and appeals for them to do something about it. The sad truth of the human tendency to delay action emerges in their response: "But the people said nothing" (verse 21).

Answering these questions has filled my life with more meaning and joy than anything that could have come from the explanations I suspect God might offer one day in heaven. My prayer is that all who read this book will hear a few of the questions God asks and look Him square in the face and answer.

CHAPTER I

The Crossroads That Lurk Behind the Bushes

"Where are you?"

Then the man and his wife heard the sound of the LORD God as he was walking in the garden in the cool of the day, and they hid from the LORD God among the trees of the garden. But the LORD God called to the man, "Where are you?" He answered, "I heard you in the garden, and I was afraid because I was naked; so I hid."

— *Genesis 3:8–10*

* * * * *

Jonah—the dog (not the prophet)—was one of several engagement gifts I presented to my wife after she said Yes. I may never forgive myself for buying her that dog. During our final year of college, my wife and I would leave Jonah inside the apartment while we went to school. During those brief moments, he managed to wreak more havoc on our apartment than a nuclear bomb could have. I'm only slightly exaggerating. On one occasion I found the contents of our cupboards scattered all over the house. Cereal littered the wood floors like pellets of hail covering the ground. Partially eaten fruits and vegetables rested comfortably on our only sofa. An empty tomato soup can nestled casually on my pillow, with most of the contents smeared over the light-blue down comforter.

When I saw the mess, the roar from my throat—the intensity of my rage—frightened even me! I called Jonah, but he didn't obey my voice. (Now you know why we called him Jonah.) I tried various tones, hoping to lure him out of hiding. I decided that he had died from a heart attack caused by my tirade or that perhaps he had gone temporarily deaf. I finally found him under the bed, and as I looked at his tomato-stained face, I saw two things: fear and shame. Fear and shame chained that sweet little puppy under the bed. Although I wanted to wring his neck, I sensed Jonah knew what he had done was wrong, but he had no idea what to do about it—other than hide.

When you mess up, perhaps the only options seem to be fight or flight. Have fear and shame ever pushed you into hiding? If so, you know what it's like when all you can think about is what you did and why you did it and what is going to happen next. The whole experience sinks into the pit of your stomach like a ton of bricks. And because when it comes to God, the "fight" option is only slightly less desirable than the "flight" option, you hide. I often wonder why it is easier to hide instead of facing up to God when we sin. Maybe the truth of our condition is too hard to admit, or perhaps it's too easy to avoid. Facing God in the moment of failure is frightening.

A friend who wrestled with an addiction to alcohol admitted to me, "I avoided the AA meetings because I had heard the horror stories of how they make you face the truth about yourself." If racing away from God allows us a reprieve from the truth, it is difficult *not* to run away. Have you considered why stealing is such an attractive option for children? I once asked a young person in juvenile detention a forthright question: "Why did you steal the CD player?"

"I wanted to get a CD player without paying for it," he answered. The short-term benefits of stealing are that you get stuff without paying for it; the long-term effects are damaging, but who looks at the long term in the moment of passion? So it is with facing the truth of your brokenness. If you can avoid your shame for a moment, maybe you can avoid it forever.

Try to imagine what it must have been like for Adam and Eve after disobeying God in the Garden of Eden. The sound of God's voice calls to them. "What will He say?" "What will He think?" "What is He going to do?" "What should we say?"

It helps to survey the key parts of the story (see Genesis 2:8–3:9). Adam and Eve are created by God and inhabit the Garden, enjoying natural communion with their Creator. But embedded in the beauty of the Garden, a dangerous foe waits for the perfect moment to impart his selfish plague to the human race. Lucifer had been banished from heaven to earth; now he makes the created children of God his primary target in order to prove to the universe that God is unfair, arbitrary, and high-handed. The cosmic contest of wills rages in the Garden; Eve is tempted by the idea of becoming like God, and Adam is tested to disobey God and be loyal to Eve. The snake plants in Eve a fatal distrust in God's word that ultimately ends in betrayal. Eve buys the lie, and Adam chooses Eve. The minions of evil slap high fives and celebrate a last-minute victory for their team. Adam and Eve, overcome by the horror of their betrayal and disobedience, hide when they hear God's footsteps in the Garden. God, of course, is keenly aware of their choice, and yet, He still comes to be with them in the Garden. And here we have God's first question to humanity: "Where are you?"

Why do we hide from an all-seeing Father and run from the only One who can help us? When we haven't prayed honestly in a while, why do we resist a conversation with God? When we have sinned, perhaps only in the inner recesses of our minds, we still hide, even though we know that God knows. Why? In the deepest part of our human experience, the thing that causes us to sin—selfishness—still reigns and tries to protect self from God's presence.

How are we going to solve the problem? Isn't hiding from God a little like refusing to see the doctor when we are injured? Not only does sin sever our relationship with God, it discourages us into believing that it's impossible to fix the problem.

The question God asked Adam and Eve is the same question that convicts the hearts of sinners all over the world today: "Where are you?" Behind the bushes of fear and shame, Adam and Eve wrestled with one of the deepest human conundrums: Do I admit my sin and ask for help? Or do I save face and try to solve the problem on my own?

The wise man once said, "There is a way that seems right to a man, / but in the end it leads to death" (Proverbs 14:12). "Trust in the LORD with all your heart / and lean not on your own understanding" (Proverbs 3:5). At the end of Solomon's life, he realized how our minds can play tricks on us. The sneakiest trick in the playbook of sin is to convince us that we can solve our own sin problems. The truth is, we *can,* but the solution is less than ideal. "The wages of sin is death," Paul tells us (Romans 6:23). And he also points out that "all have sinned and fall short of the glory of God" (Romans 3:23). Sin costs, and there is no way around it other than paying the price.

There are two ways to deal with your sin. You can pay for it yourself (wages of sin = death), or you can have Someone pay for you ("while we were still sinners, Christ died for us" [Romans 5:8]). Either way, someone has to die to pay for your sin. The question is, Who pays for you?

Standing at the crossroads of life and death, Adam and Eve hid behind the bushes. It was their decision. Face the One who knows your shame; or hide from God and resolve to fix the sin problem yourself, somehow, someway. What does it look like when you come out from behind the bushes for help?

- Pray the long-awaited, honest prayer and pour it all out in detail.
- Step forward at the altar call.
- Ask a trusted friend to help you find help for your secret addiction.
- Write the person you hate a letter of forgiveness.
- Invite a faithful believer to pray with you.
- Admit to your spouse, child, or parent that you were wrong.

Admitting our sin is exposure, a point of no return. A student came to my office, dancing with small talk before he launched into full disclosure: "I'm struggling with pornography." You can't go back and redefine that one or say, "I was just kidding." You can't explain it away. It can't be misconstrued as miscommunication. It's simply too honest to rationalize. But ask anyone who breaks the silence of their sin, with God or others, and they'll tell you that it's liberating to come clean.

What does it look like when you try to hide and fix the problem yourself?

- Work incessantly—look and act busy.
- Focus on the failures of people around you.
- Distract yourself with a social life.
- Talk with others about only meaningless things and for only short periods of time.
- Immerse yourself in long periods of escape (movies, sports, novels, Internet).

- Engage in temporary, feel-good exercises, such as sex or shopping.
- Hang around people who don't talk about or care about how lost and empty you are.
- Attach yourself to people with whom you will never be challenged to truly connect.

Were Adam and Eve really hiding from God? Did God not know where they were? Did sin somehow interrupt the global positioning device in God's mind? God knew where they were. Adam and Eve were afraid because the implications of their disobedience began to dawn on them. The words of the Creator echoed in their minds: " 'You are free to eat from any tree in the garden; but you must not eat from the tree of the knowledge of good and evil, for when you eat of it you will surely die' " (Genesis 2:16, 17). God knew that His children were alone and lost—eternally. Their sin separated them from life beyond their relatively innocent comprehension. The reason God called to them in the Garden asking "Where are you?" (Genesis 3:9) is that the question is monumental, a matter of life and death. The answer can be either, "I'm here, hiding, full of shame and fear, and in need of help," or it can be, "I'm just fine. Don't worry about me; I will be all right on my own."

I've often thought that being blind would be awful. But imagine being blind and thinking that you can see just fine. At least the blind use a dog, a cane, or some form of help. The blind who think they can see are out of reach of help. William Barclay claims that the sins that God despises most are the ones that put us out of His reach to save—hypocrisy, self-sufficiency, and self-righteousness.* What makes God sick to His stomach about Laodicea becomes a striking indictment to all who are blind but think they see just fine: " 'You say, "I am rich; I have acquired wealth and do not need a thing." But you do not realize that you are wretched, pitiful, poor, blind and naked' " (Revelation 3:17). It is when you realize that you are in need of a Savior that salvation can come. How hard it is, though, to be saved when you see no need for help.

---

* William Barclay, *The Mind of Jesus* (New York: HarperCollins, 1960), 127, 128.

When Adam and Eve stepped forward from the bushes, God had already begun the work of redemption. Of course, there were the questions: "What did you do?" "Who told you that you were naked?" "Have you eaten from the tree that I commanded you not to eat from?" Although God knew the answers to all these questions, Adam and Eve needed to say the words that decried the work of sin to the coming centuries.

Right before their eyes and with their own hands, the sacrifice is made. For the first time in the history of the universe, the blood of a living creature falls to the ground, only hinting at the true cost of sin. In that moment Adam and Eve chose between two options. They could pay for their sin, or they could let Someone pay for them. Sometime later the Lamb, the One hoped for in the Garden, hung on the cross. Although the sight of blood was familiar to humanity by that time, the angels and a few others witnessed *the event* that the sacrifice of Eden pointed to. Someone had to pay. Paul says,

> Consequently, just as the result of one trespass was condemnation for all men, so also the result of one act of righteousness was justification that brings life for all men. For just as through the disobedience of the one man the many were made sinners, so also through the obedience of the one man the many will be made righteous (Romans 5:18, 19).

> [And so] Christ's love compels us, because we are convinced that one died for all, and therefore all died (2 Corinthians 5:14).

Where are you? God calls to each heart hiding behind whatever bushes we take cover in. Will you resist God's call to you? Or will you step out of the bushes and lay hold of the Father, who has already made a better way for you to deal with your sin? You may recall the words of Christ Himself: " 'Come to me, all you who are weary and burdened, and I will give you rest' " (Matthew 11:28). At least seventeen times in the Gospels Jesus implores people to come to Him.

Or maybe you are still afraid of how the Father might react to your admission of guilt. Jesus says,

"Whoever comes to me I will never drive away. For I have come down from heaven not to do my will but to do the will of him who sent me. And this is the will of him who sent me, that I shall lose none of all that he has given me, but raise them up at the last day. For my Father's will is that everyone who looks to the Son and believes in him shall have eternal life, and I will raise him up at the last day" (John 6:37–40).

God's question reveals His heart and His will for your life. What does the question "Where are you?" convey about God's heart? It conveys the *almost* unbelievable love He has displayed in His willingness to embrace you and deal with your shame by paying for it Himself. What does this question say about God's will for your life? It says that He wants to establish the intimacy of the Garden again.

But you must respond. From wherever you are and from wherever you have been, answer His call. Answer His question with a prayer, a song, a thought, a letter, a heartfelt confession, a truckload of tears, or shouts of joy—just answer. Step out from behind the bushes and answer God's first question: "Where are you?"

Questions for Reflection and Study

1. Has fear and shame ever pushed you into hiding? How did that situation resolve itself? What were the consequences—short term, or long term?
2. When we do something we shouldn't, why do you think our first thought is to hide? Does trying to hide usually prove helpful?
3. In what areas of your life do you find it most difficult to relinquish control to God?
4. If you completely gave your entire life over to God, what do you think He would ask you to change about the way you live? Would you be willing to make that change?
5. What are the implications for your life of realizing that God already knows "where you are"—every detail of what is going on in your life? How does that make you feel?

CHAPTER 2

Missed or Taken Identity

"Where are your accusers?"

Jesus went to the Mount of Olives. At dawn he appeared again in the temple courts, where all the people gathered around him, and he sat down to teach them. The teachers of the law and the Pharisees brought in a woman caught in adultery. They made her stand before the group and said to Jesus, "Teacher, this woman was caught in the act of adultery. In the Law Moses commanded us to stone such women. Now what do you say?" They were using this question as a trap, in order to have a basis for accusing him.

But Jesus bent down and started to write on the ground with his finger. When they kept on questioning him, he straightened up and said to them, "If any one of you is without sin, let him be the first to throw a stone at her." Again he stooped down and wrote on the ground.

At this, those who heard began to go away one at a time, the older ones first, until only Jesus was left, with the woman still standing there. Jesus straightened up and asked her, "Woman, where are they? Has no one condemned you?"

"No one, sir," she said.

"Then neither do I condemn you," Jesus declared. "Go now and leave your life of sin."

— John 8:1–11

* * * * *

In the book *Don't Just Stand There, Pray Something,** Ronald Dunn tells the story of a woman leaving a shopping mall in search of her car. Arriving at her car, she discovers the keys resting safely in the ignition and her doors, of course, locked. Thinking about a pie she left in the oven at home, she frantically seeks to get in. She races into the mall in search of a wire coat hanger, because everyone knows that a coat hanger can unlock a car. With a look of grim determination she bursts out of the mall again with a wire coat hanger. Not really knowing what to do, but being a woman of faith, she begins to pray. Within a minute a man comes her way. Unkempt hair. Unshaven. Tattooed. He's wearing torn jeans and a T-shirt riddled with holes. While he might have looked dangerous to some, she sees something different.

"Do you know how to use one of these?" she asks, holding the coat hanger out to him.

He looks suspiciously at her. Is this a trick?

She explains. "My keys are locked in the car, and I need to get home. I left a pie in the oven."

With a heroic look on his face, he snatches the coat hanger from her hand and springs to the driver's door with catlike dexterity. Like a skilled engineer, he shapes the coat hanger into a precision tool. It is as if he has done this for a living. With a few quick, fluid movements the lock pops, he opens the door, and presents the open car to her with a graceful bow.

She is so filled with awe at this man's skill that she bursts out, "Praise God! You are such a good man. You must be a Christian."

Looking down sheepishly, he replies, "Ma'am, I'm not a good man, and I'm definitely not a Christian. I just got out of jail for stealing cars."

Without missing a beat, she exclaims, "Well, praise God, He sent me a professional!"

Perhaps you know someone like this, a person who sees the most positive virtues in anyone. Most of the time we do not see the best in people; we see the worst. If there are two truths that are embedded deep within

---

* Ronald Dunn, *Don't Just Stand There, Pray Something* (San Bernardino, Calif.: Here's Life Publishers, 1991), 21–23.

our human experience, they are our need for justice and our love of mercy. We love justice when someone who deserves it gets it, and we embrace mercy when we, who need it, receive it.

For example, consider a few convicted felons walking the streets today: Gregory Wallis served seventeen years of a fifty-year sentence; Michael Anthony Williams served twenty-three years of a life sentence; and Alejandro Fernandez served ten years of a death sentence. How does it make you feel to know these men were convicted of violent crimes and served only less than half their time?

They are currently out on the street walking free today—as they should be. These men were released, not prematurely, but much later than they should have been because they were convicted based upon mistaken identity and, in some cases, false testimony. It was only after new technology with DNA testing and the earnest effort of an organization called the Innocence Project that they were exonerated. Recently, more than two hundred people who were falsely convicted, sentenced, and served time have been set free.

Our hunger for justice and our love for mercy are core to who we are as humans. Think of the stories from your life when you experienced grace, and also consider the moments when you stood passionately on the side of justice. What is the connection, if any, between these two experiences? If there was ever an event in the Bible that conveyed a message of both justice and mercy, it's in the eighth chapter of John's Gospel. Several things in this story emerge and call for careful attention.

First, Jesus is teaching early in the morning in the temple courts, where the very laws and systems of learning about salvation were taught and executed. Second, according to Jewish law, anyone who is an eyewitness must cast the first stone. It's one thing to accuse someone of a crime that merits death, but it is a sobering experience to become part of the execution process.

Dealing with false witnesses demanded the following action: "The judges must make a thorough investigation, and if the witness proves to be a liar, giving false testimony against his brother, then do to him as he intended to do to his brother" (Deuteronomy 19:18, 19). Furthermore, it is the husband's duty to bring the charges—not the over-religious "Peeping Toms" in town.

Another fact important to this story is that all parties involved in adultery must die, as stated in Leviticus 20:10: " 'If a man commits adultery with another man's wife—with the wife of his neighbor—both the adulterer and the adulteress must be put to death.' "

But Jesus, presented with this seemingly complicated problem, solves it by leveling the playing field, saying in a sense, "OK, if you want to play by the letter of the law, then let's look at *all* the letters." So Jesus penned all the letters applying to everyone's life on the ground for the whole community to see.

Clearly, this whole event had nothing to do with the woman other than she was a perfect pawn to use against Jesus. But then Jesus declares, "Anyone who is without sin, let him cast the first stone." This is the rule, and it was uncommon to the crowd. Perhaps the most penetrating feature of this scene is that *everyone* is exposed for who they really are. The woman is an adulteress, broken and abused, but still a sinner. The sinfulness of the religious leaders is unveiled; truth demands they drop their rocks and leave. Everyone leaves because, even though they may not be adulterers, they had probably wanted to be at one point or another. Ellen White portrays this scene in *The Desire of Ages:*

> These would-be guardians of justice had themselves led their victim into sin, that they might lay a snare for Jesus. . . .
>
> But as their eyes, following those of Jesus, fell upon the pavement at His feet, their countenances changed. There, traced before them, were the guilty secrets of their own lives. The people, looking on, saw the sudden change of expression, and pressed forward to discover what it was that they were regarding with such astonishment and shame.*

There were not enough stones in the courtyard that morning to mete out justice for everyone who deserved it. As this became evident to all, one at a time they left, from the oldest to the youngest.

---

* Ellen G. White, *The Desire of Ages* (Mountain View, Calif.: Pacific Press® Publishing Association, 1940), 461.

The high point of this story is how gloriously Jesus is unveiled as the Son of God, who demands justice and delivers mercy. He never minimizes the sin of the woman because "the wages of sin" is still death, and someone needs to pay. But Jesus, in view of His own sacrifice, dismisses her case because He is soon to stand in her place and die. No one on earth is more aware of the price of sin than is Christ. In fact, self-righteousness could be one of the most despicable sins because it is so hard to save someone who doesn't believe he or she needs to be saved.

On that particular morning, the courtyard empties and, after everyone else has gone, Jesus asks the woman life-changing questions: "Where are your accusers? Is there anyone who condemns you?"

What do these questions tell us about Christ? We want Him judging us because He will be just. We want Him judging us because, even though He knows the worst about us, He wants the best for us.

As in the case of this woman caught in the act of adultery, Christ offers her an opportunity to take on a new identity. What is her answer to the life-splitting questions? "No one, sir."

But there is an obstacle that often gets in the way of our certainty of salvation, our walk of freedom, and the realization that in Christ no one condemns us—and that is *reality*. I want to believe with surety that God's grace and mercy will save me, but I know the worst about me, and I know God knows. That is the reality check. Because while I would love to receive mercy, I also have a sense of what is just. Such knowledge makes believing in the grace of God one of the most difficult things to do. Belief that keeping all the rules and regulations—the life of legalism—is ten times easier than the leap of faith required for us to rest in God's mercy. Perhaps the notion that salvation is free sticks in the throat of the cynic because inside all of us, we know nothing is free. Knowing what salvation costs and who paid it is what makes the experience valuable and real. Furthermore, nothing cripples our walk with God like failing to answer the question, "Where are your accusers?" To answer this question we must fully trust in the judgment process of heaven; and though some might instantly accept this ruling on our behalf, for others it might take a little more time.

As I have sat at the bedside of saints who watch death draw close, I've noticed some are confident of their eternal home in heaven while others quake at the notion that they might not have their names written in the book of life. Some simply stare at their inconsistent track record of devotion to God and are overcome with doubt. Sometimes we are alive and responsive, and then there are the valleys—those seasons of disinterest or weakness.

The question Jesus asks opens up a whole series of other questions we must negotiate through in order to give Him a response:

- How can we ever feel sure about our salvation with such a tumultuous walk with God?
- Knowing that Christ knows our worst but believes the best, how do we walk in confidence?
- How does this "Go and sin no more" principle really work?

First, whether we feel right about this or not, taking on a new identity involves a choice. We must choose.

The woman had to choose to believe that she had just gone from death to life. She had to believe it and receive it. "Where are your accusers?" If we want to feel saved, we must choose to believe it is true and say the words: "No one condemns who can, and the only One who can condemn me is taking my place." The act of receiving this gift has been a conundrum for many, as John records: "He was in the world, and though the world was made through him, the world did not recognize him. He came to that which was his own, but his own did not receive him. Yet to all who received him, to those who believed in his name, he gave the right to become children of God—children born not of natural descent, nor of human decision or a husband's will, but born of God" (John 1:10–13).

I began to understand the transition from despair to confidence when I was working at a summer camp in Yosemite National Park. The cowboy campers had set out on a trail ride to a beautiful meadow where the campers would spend the night under the stars. I drove the old camp pickup truck out to the meadow in order to eat a meal and sing a few songs with the kids. Through the trees I could see the young people milling around as they checked to make sure the horses were tied up correctly. As I walked by one particular horse, I smelled something strange. Even though I stood amid eighteen sweaty horses, I followed the scent to the side of one horse and found the saddle soaking wet. I didn't need to get closer to deduce that someone wet the horse.

My mind raced through the list of teens on the pack trip, and none of them had medical issues or anything I could think of. Then it dawned on me; there was a ten-year-old boy (we'll call him Joshua), who joined the teens on the pack trip. I scanned the meadow and located Joshua, standing in line holding a stainless steel tray in front of him with his legs crossed and looking apprehensive. If any of those teen boys knew what had happened, there was no telling of the shame that could have been inflicted with a few careless jibes. I moved quickly to the line and stood between Joshua and the other campers and said, "Joshua, we need to talk for a moment, can you walk with me, please?" I guided the scared lad into the meadow away from the others, and as soon as we were out of range, the tears began to stream down his dusty face.

I asked, "Joshua, what happened? Why did you . . . wet the horse?"

The dam of despair and shame broke, and he sobbed uncontrollably, "I had to go . . . and the uh, uh, uh, girls were right there . . . and uh, uh, uh, the bears were . . ."

At the beginning of camp we told all the kids not to go into the forest alone because of bears. Now the teens took such warnings a different way than a ten-year-old did. Furthermore, more frightful than any bear would be the presence of a teen girl anywhere within a hundred yards of the natural facilities in the woods. He had to go but was too embarrassed to say so in front of the girls and too frightened by a trek into the forest; trapped in his predicament, he wet the horse.

I tried to find a way to get a change of clothes for him, but the sun was setting and he was wearing the only clothes he had, except back at camp. Then I heard the sound of the creek about twenty-five yards behind us, and I took him to the stream. There, I bent over the water and splashed him with a spray of cold creek water, and he squealed, "Hey, you're getting me all wet!" We splashed each other back and forth. I found a space in the creek deep enough to really get him wet. I wrestled him around in the creek for a bit, staying upstream, of course, and occasionally simulating a spin cycle in the water until he was soaking wet. We both walked back to the camp completely covered. Josh was saved from his shame, and when the others inquired as to what happened to us, we simply said, "We got wet."

Perhaps this is what Paul meant when he said: "Christ's love compels us, because we are convinced that one died for all, and therefore all died. . . . Therefore, if anyone is in Christ, he is a new creation; the old has gone, the new has come. . . . God made him who had no sin to be sin for us, so that in him we might become the righteousness of God" (2 Corinthians 5:14–21).

Choose to believe it's true. Decide that no matter how you feel, what you have done, or even what you might know God knows about you—His mercy is real. And receiving that mercy is a choice you make to believe it's true.

The second stage in becoming confident in our walk with God has to do with how we talk about what we have chosen. We need to *profess shamelessly* our new standing in Christ in every way we possibly can. John affirms this activity saying,

That which was from the beginning, which we have heard, which we have seen with our eyes, which we have looked at and our hands have touched—this we proclaim concerning the Word of life. The life appeared; we have seen it and testify to it, and we proclaim to you the eternal life, which was with the Father and has appeared to us. We proclaim to you what we have seen and heard, so that you also may have fellowship with us. And our fellowship is with the Father and with his Son, Jesus Christ. We write this to make our joy complete (1 John 1:1–4).

Speak it. Say it. Declare it. Even if it doesn't entirely make sense, profess what God says is true about our identity: I am a child of God. Free. Reborn. Perfect in Him. I think we need to accept the fact we may not always feel this way. Maybe this is why Jesus asked the woman a question with such an obvious answer. Perhaps there is power in just saying it aloud. Answering this question out loud may have more impact than you might initially imagine.

"Is there anyone here who is accusing you?"

"No one, sir."

A young man who had been adopted shared with me how weird it was saying his new name. Shifting from one foster care home to another, he was finally adopted by a family that gave him a new life and a new name—Kyle O'Conner. "At first it was kind of strange," he said, "but the more I heard my own voice say it—'Kyle O'Conner'—the more I began to believe that I had a new life."

Finally, as you choose to believe and shamelessly profess what God has done for you, *walk intentionally with Him,* working out this salvation in you as Paul urges:

> My dear friends, as you have always obeyed—not only in my presence, but now much more in my absence—continue to work out your salvation with fear and trembling, for it is God who works in you to will and to act according to his good purpose (Philippians 2:12, 13).

Work it out. Practice. Walk. Live. Give. Share. Work. Sing. Serve. Pray. Jesus commanded the woman, "Go, and sin no more." Go and live differently—not in spite of your failures but in the pure light of your new identity: not guilty!

The story is told of a melancholy lawyer who moved to a new town to begin a new law practice. Townspeople often observed him walking by himself in the evening with his head bowed and his posture stooped. One day he confessed to an artist that in his past he had made a critical mistake that he just couldn't shake. The failure haunted him. The artist said nothing, but a few weeks later he invited the dejected lawyer to view a portrait in his studio. The lawyer accepted, and when he looked at the painting, he was surprised to see a portrait of himself, except that in the portrait, he stood tall and confident, with his head held high. Ambition, vision, and courage were written all over his face in the portrait. After taking in this vision of what the artist could see, a vision of what he could become was born in his heart. The lawyer told himself, "If the artist can see that in me, then I can see it too. If he thinks that I can be that man, then I will be that man." Every day the lawyer saw the portrait, and over time his demeanor changed.

As we choose to believe in God's grace for us, profess it, and walk and live in the light of God's view of us, our confidence in the justice and mercy of God will increase.

Maybe experiencing the assurance of salvation is a lot like making a cup of tea. I offered to teach the young people how to make a cup of tea. "First, you get a cup of hot water and a tea bag. Next, you dip the bag into the water . . . and you take it out." The young people murmured, "No, you have to leave it in longer." Sure enough, very little color or flavor was evident in the water. So, I left it in for five seconds. "No, . . . longer," they cried. A few wisps of color began to leak out of the bag and into the water. But by leaving the bag in the water over time, the flavor and the color of the water significantly changed.

As we get into the truth, this almost unbelievable truth of God's justice and mercy, the good news saturates us, and our confidence grows as we choose to believe it, profess it, and walk in it. Like the woman, we can go and leave the identity behind and take on a new one. Becoming accustomed to the new name and standing takes time and some effort. But it is real.

Whenever I struggle to live with certainty about my standing in Christ, I reflect on a moment in my childhood when I played in a soccer tournament against the Minute Men. These boys were older, faster, stronger, and had a diverse vocabulary that would intimidate most young scholars. They tripped, pushed, jeered, and pummeled my team into the turf. We were going to lose. At the half, my coach gathered the team together in order to give us a pep talk. Pep talks were never helpful to me, especially when filled with empty clichés, such as, "You are all winners" or "Whatever happens out there, just give your best" or "It's not important whether you win or lose, but whether you have fun." We weren't winning and our best wasn't good enough and it wasn't fun. So, when our coach started with "I want you all to know that whatever happens in the second half, you are all first-place winners," I rolled my eyes and let out a gasp of frustration. "I'm serious, you guys," our coach pleaded, "you are winners!"

I retorted, "The scoreboard says three to zero and unless I'm counting wrong, we are going to lose."

The coach added, "I realize that, but what you don't realize is that the team you are playing isn't even in your league or your division. Furthermore, some of their players vandalized the tournament facility and, as a result, their team, although they are on the field, has been disqualified. You have already won! Your name is on the trophy!"

We all glanced over to the covered table on the side of the field that hid the awards that would be presented at the end of the game.

The coach said, "I didn't want to tell you this until halftime. But I'm telling you now, go out there and play like you have won."

In a way, this is the message Christ had for the woman caught in adultery. But in order for her to truly walk away with a new identity, she had to answer the question Jesus asked, "Where are your accusers?" When we answer that question, we are ushered into a new world where we believe fully and walk confidently in the mercy given to us. "Go, and sin no more" is a command to live in the knowledge that we have already won.

Questions for Reflection and Study

1. Are your most insistent accusers internal or external?
2. Do you agree with this statement: "Most people get what they deserve in life"? Why, or why not?
3. Why do you think Jesus refused to condemn the woman taken in adultery—when she was obviously guilty? What does this say about Jesus? What does it say about the woman?
4. Could society function if it were to operate on God's principle of grace? Why, or why not? Is there one standard for individuals and another for society as a whole in the way we relate to those who are guilty of breaking the law?
5. Do you find it easier to accept grace or to give grace? Why?

CHAPTER 3

Un-Useless Love

"If you love those who love you, what good is that?"

"I tell you who hear me: Love your enemies, do good to those who hate you, bless those who curse you, pray for those who mistreat you. If someone strikes you on one cheek, turn to him the other also. If someone takes your cloak, do not stop him from taking your tunic. Give to everyone who asks you, and if anyone takes what belongs to you, do not demand it back. Do to others as you would have them do to you.

"If you love those who love you, what credit is that to you? Even 'sinners' love those who love them. And if you do good to those who are good to you, what credit is that to you? Even 'sinners' do that. And if you lend to those from whom you expect repayment, what credit is that to you? Even 'sinners' lend to 'sinners,' expecting to be repaid in full. But love your enemies, do good to them, and lend to them without expecting to get anything back. Then your reward will be great, and you will be sons of the Most High, because he is kind to the ungrateful and wicked. Be merciful, just as your Father is merciful."

— Luke 6:27–36

*   *   *   *   *

Chindohgu is the Japanese art of the un-useless invention. These creations are un-useless because at first they seem absurd but have a quirky way of getting the job done. For example, there's the latex finger glove with bristles for those moments when you forget your toothbrush and need to use your finger. Another *chindohgu* features a small battery operated fan that attaches to a pair of chopsticks to cool your noodles as you eat (I have almost hyperventilated cooling my noodles). Still another invention that had to have made the list of top-ten *chindohgus* is an apparatus you attach to a car that functions as a clothesline, so as you drive around town you can dry your wet laundry.

Perhaps my favorite creation is the duster slippers made of mop material that would be worn on all four paws of a common house cat. Cat slippers that mop the dust from the floor or anywhere the cat chooses to venture. One might enhance the effectiveness of that invention by including some bonus samples of caffeinated catnip and really speed up the cleaning process.

Chindohgu inventions are really more of an art culture than entrepreneurial endeavors. But what intrigued me most about *chindohgus* had to do with the way an irrational and seemingly useless idea had taken hold of me. The more I thought about each one, the more absurd it seemed.

Some of the things Jesus said shock and twist our thinking, and if we have no patience with what He is saying, it falls away. But if we stop and allow these hard sayings to marinate in our mind a bit, a truth so real and meaningful tends to emerge.

Consider a few classic lines from Jesus: " 'I tell you the truth, anyone who has faith in me will do what I have been doing. He will do even greater things than these, because I am going to the Father' " (John 14:12). " 'Whoever wants to save his life will lose it, but whoever loses his life for me will save it' " (Luke 9:24). " 'I tell you that anyone who is angry with his brother will be subject to judgment. Again, anyone who says to his brother, "Raca," is answerable to the Sanhedrin. But anyone who says, "You fool!" will be in danger of the fire of hell' " (Matthew 5:22). " 'I tell you the truth: Among those born of women there has not risen anyone greater than John the Baptist; yet he who is least in the kingdom of heaven is greater than he' " (Matthew 11:11).

F. F. Bruce, in *The Hard Sayings of Jesus*, observes that statements like these are difficult:

> For to us there are two kinds of hard sayings: there are some which are hard to understand, and there are some which are only

too easy to understand. When sayings of Jesus which are hard in the former sense are explained in dynamically equivalent terms, then they are likely to become hard in the latter sense. Mark Twain spoke for many when he said that the things in the Bible that bothered him were not those that he did not understand but those that he did understand. This is particularly true of the sayings of Jesus. The better we understand them, the harder they are to take.*

There is one statement that is both hard to explain and hard to do. This nine-word sentence tops the list of the hard sayings of Jesus, " 'Be perfect, therefore, as your heavenly Father is perfect' " (Matthew 5:48).

A first reading of this statement stonewalls those who hear it because it seems irrational and impossible. Jesus has to be kidding, or He must mean something else! He can't possibly think we could achieve this perfection. So we are compelled to assume that Jesus simply wants us to try to be like God anyway, and the exercise of trying will keep us humble and somewhat moral in the process. This interpretation is absolutely foolish when you think about it, because no one is going to mindlessly try to do the impossible and, furthermore, he or she won't be a better person because of it.

There is no way to look at this phrase metaphorically, which is why it is so disturbing. But this command does not stand alone; it is set up by a series of questions that may help us make sense out of it. Many of the hardest sayings of Jesus are framed by a question or series of questions that prompt, expand, or explain an abrupt statement.

When Christ commands His followers to "be perfect," He builds a case to respond with four sequential questions that establish the command:

- If you love those who love you, what reward will you get?
- Are not even the tax collectors doing that?
- And if you greet only your brothers, what are you doing more than others?
- Do not even pagans do that?

---

* F. F. Bruce, *The Hard Sayings of Jesus* (Downers Grove, Ill.: InterVarsity Press, 1983), 16, 17.

When you look carefully at the meaning of the word *perfect* and its application in the previous questions, what Christ calls believers to do is both reasonable and possible. The questions unveil three qualities of perfect love.

First, perfect love is mature. Barclay discusses the meaning of the word *teleos* or *perfect*, noting that a man who reaches full-grown stature is *teleos* in comparison to a child. A student who graduates with a mature knowledge is *teleos* in contrast to a student just starting school. It is vital to note that *perfect* does not mean "flawless" but "full-grown."*

After spending a weekend at a very moving religious rally, a student came to me with a renewed passion for being perfect in every aspect of his life. It became clear that the presenters pounded this young man with enough fear and shame to bring him to a place of conviction but gave him very little insight as to how to actually work toward perfection.

I asked, "So, what are you going to do to start this endeavor?" He replied quickly, "Well, I stopped watching TV and torched my music that put impure thoughts in my mind, and I told my friends (the ones that tend to bring me down), that I wasn't going to hang out with them anymore."

Everything he mentioned seemed to be a good idea, but his response totally missed the point of perfection. In the biblical sense, perfection isn't about what you abstain from or avoid as much as it is about what you embrace. In other words, perfect love is not about what you don't do but is something you actively do. What Jesus says is that perfect love has to do with how you proactively behave toward the people who harm or disrespect you. So I tried to explain this principle to the young man, but it was evident that I was not getting through the way others got through to him about perfection. So, I handed him a bottle of water.

I said, "Look at the ingredients and tell me what is *not* in the water."

He immediately turned the bottle over and paused thoughtfully, then smiled and sat back in the chair looking up into the ceiling shaking his head.

---

* William Barclay, *The Gospel of Matthew*, vol. 1 (Philadelphia: Westminster Press, 1975), 177.

"I think I get it," he said. When something is considered pure, it actually means "having only one ingredient." Again, Jesus' call to perfect love is a journey to something you do, not something you don't do.

Even though there are sects of Christians who have purposed themselves toward a life of flawlessness, they, too, miss the mark. But a believer is mature—perfect—when he or she *acts graciously, gives generously, thinks compassionately, and prays faithfully for the person who is hard to pray for.*

A second quality revealed in the questions Jesus asked is that perfect love is effective. Something is *teleos,* or perfect, if it realizes the purpose for which it is planned. We are perfect when we realize the purpose for which we are created. If you have a screw loose (and some suggest this is true on many levels), what is needed is a screwdriver that fits. The handle may not be your favorite color; it may not even fit the grip of your hand well; in fact, the tip may be dull or not even the exact size of the head of the screw. But if the screwdriver effectively tightens the screw, it is *teleos.* Functional. Effective. Useful toward its intended purpose.

At the end of life's journey, there are many who regret the course of their life because they sense they had a greater purpose to live for than the one they chose. Then there are others who may have specific regrets about misdeeds or missed opportunities, but have peace about how their life served a purpose that was noble.

Consider the apostle Paul in his final moments, not a flawless man by any means but perfect in meaning: "I have fought the good fight, I have finished the race, I have kept the faith" (2 Timothy 4:7). Paul had peace about how he fulfilled an effective, meaningful purpose in life. His confidence echoes the perfection Christ is calling His followers to, saying, " 'Love your enemies and pray for those who persecute you, that you may be sons of your Father in heaven' " (1 John 3:1). How great is the love the Father has lavished on us, that we should be called children of God! And that is what we are!

Read this passage from Ephesians and note the glorious purpose for which we were created and redeemed:

> Praise be to the God and Father of our Lord Jesus Christ, who
> has blessed us in the heavenly realms with every spiritual blessing

in Christ. For he chose us in him before the creation of the world to be holy and blameless in his sight. In love he predestined us to be adopted as his sons through Jesus Christ, in accordance with his pleasure and will—to the praise of his glorious grace, which he has freely given us in the One he loves. In him we have redemption through his blood, the forgiveness of sins, in accordance with the riches of God's grace that he lavished on us with all wisdom and understanding. And he made known to us the mystery of his will according to his good pleasure, which he purposed in Christ, to be put into effect when the times will have reached their fulfillment—to bring all things in heaven and on earth together under one head, even Christ.

In him we were also chosen, having been predestined according to the plan of him who works out everything in conformity with the purpose of his will, in order that we, who were the first to hope in Christ, might be for the praise of his glory. And you also were included in Christ when you heard the word of truth, the gospel of your salvation. Having believed, you were marked in him with a seal, the promised Holy Spirit, who is a deposit guaranteeing our inheritance until the redemption of those who are God's possession—to the praise of his glory (Ephesians 1:3–14).

It is important to mark our purpose in light of creation and redemption, because our redemption assumes we are anything but flawless. But the overarching mood of the passage is a beautiful picture of God's ultimate purpose for us.

Finally, the questions Jesus asks capture the way *perfect love is remarkable*. According to Jesus, ordinary human love is expected, while extraordinary love is distinct and can come only from godlike behavior.

"You have heard that it was said, 'Love your neighbor and hate your enemy.' But I tell you: Love your enemies and pray for those who persecute you, that you may be sons of your Father in heaven. . . . If you love those who love you, what reward will you get? Are not even the tax collectors doing that? And if you greet only your brothers, what are you doing more than others? Do not even pagans do that?" (Matthew 5:43–47).

The word for "love" in this passage does not convey friendship, affection, or passion. Agape love is what William Barclay refers to as an "unconquerable benevolence" and "invincible good will—to seek their highest good no matter who they are or what they do to us."*

Jesus never asks us to love our enemies in the same way we love our parents, friends, or mates. Agape love extends grace and goodwill to people who don't deserve it and, in many cases, are not even asking for it.

I don't know a parent alive today—believer or seeker or cynic—who does not love his children to the degree he would give his own life to save his child. This is a common basic feature of people who are created in the image of God.

Jesus claims, "That's easy"—so what makes you different from the rest of the world? How does God's glorious face shine through you in ways that mark you as a child of heaven?

In 1995 a remarkable thing happened:

A scene occurred in Burma, now called Myanmar, that fifty years earlier no one could have ever imagined. It happened at the bridge over the Kwai River. During World War II the Japanese army had forced Allied prisoners of war from Britain, Australia, and the Netherlands to build a railroad. The Japanese soldiers committed many atrocities, and some sixteen thousand Allied POWs died building what has been called Death Railway. But after the war, a former Japanese army officer named Nagase Takashi went on a personal campaign to urge his government to admit the atrocities committed. After many years of effort, the result of his crusade was a brief ceremony in 1995 at the infamous bridge. On one side of the bridge were fifty Japanese, including five war veterans, and Mr. Takashi. Eighteen schoolteachers from Japan

* William Barclay, *The Gospel of Matthew*, 173.

carried two hundred letters written by children expressing sadness for what had happened during the war.

At the other side of the bridge were representatives of the Allied soldiers: Two soldiers from Britain who declared the business of fifty years ago finished at last; a young woman from Australia who came to deliver, posthumously, her father's forgiveness; a son of a POW who came to do the same; and there was seventy-three-year-old Australian David Barrett, who said he made the pilgrimage because he felt that to continue hating would destroy him. The two groups began to walk the narrow planks of the black iron bridge toward one another. When they met in the center, they shook hands, embraced, shed tears. Yuko Ikebuchi, a schoolteacher, handed the letters from the Japanese children to the veterans, and in tears turned and ran without a word.*

Such a story captures the face of God in an unmistakable, ultimately remarkable way. Perfect. Perhaps what Jesus is saying in this passage is that people will never be more perfect than when they extend unwarranted goodwill and benevolence. We might resemble God in many ways, but loving our enemies conveys the face of God with vivid clarity.

When I look at my children's baby pictures, I can't tell who those kids look like, but as they grow and mature, their faces bear undeniable resemblance to Mom and Dad. So it is with us. We are perfect, most like our Father in heaven when we take the same high road in the way we relate to our enemies. Jesus would also add, " 'By this all men will know that you are my disciples, if you love one another' " (John 13:35).

So, is it reasonable to expect people to love their enemies? Stephen Olford tells the story of Peter Miller, who lived in Ephrata, Pennsylvania, and enjoyed the friendship of George Washington.† Also in Ephrata lived a man named Michael Whitman, an evil-minded sort who did all he

---

* Christopher Tomas, "Old Foes Cross a Bridge to Forgiveness," *Times of London,* August 16, 1995, sec. 1, 1.

† Cited in Craig Brian Larson, *750 Engaging Illustrations for Preachers, Teachers, and Writers* (Grand Rapids, Mich.: Baker Books, 2002), 235.

could to oppose and humiliate the pastor. One day Michael was arrested for treason and sentenced to die. Peter Miller traveled seventy miles on foot to Philadelphia to plead for the life of the traitor.

"No, Peter," General Washington said, "I cannot grant you the life of your friend."

"My friend?" exclaimed the old preacher. "He's the bitterest enemy I have."

"What?" cried Washington. "You've walked seventy miles to save the life of an enemy? That puts the matter in a different light. I'll grant your pardon."

And he did. Peter Miller took Michael Whitman back home to Ephrata, no longer an enemy but a friend.

No act deepens the impact of the Christian faith more. If this kind of love for enemies were not possible, the story of Calvary would have long been forgotten and erased from history because what keeps the story of Christ alive were ordinary believers who acted like God to their enemies, which fostered even more to believe in God and the risen Christ.

Yes. It not only makes sense—the *only* people who could possibly love their enemies are those who have drunk so deeply in the well of grace themselves. When we consider how God forgives us, we become firsthand believers in the power of grace and the only ones for whom this kind of grace makes sense.

Furthermore, is it possible for followers of Christ to demonstrate such love?

Sergei Kourdakov was the leader of a secret KGB police force in the Soviet Union. This elite squad of youth terrorized Christians who met secretly for prayer and Bible study. Sergei grew up as an orphan in the children's homes operated by the state and proved himself to be the model Communist. He developed into a brilliant leader, and his devotion to Communism caused him to be promoted to the elite police squad. As Sergei's squad raided homes where believers gathered, he began to notice a trend that bothered him. He had been told that the only ones who subscribed to the foolish Christian faith were old, ignorant people. But with each raid, he noticed more young people professing their belief in Christ. In the quiet moments, he secretly admired their devotion and, although he was intrigued by their poise and courage, his confusion turned to anger.

Sergei and his men stormed a house full of young believers where they beat and mocked the believers as they were praying to God. The brutal leader looked on approvingly as Victor, the biggest and strongest man in his posse, lifted a young woman above his head and threw her against the wall. As she crumpled to the ground, Sergei laughed, "I'll bet the idea of God went flying out of her head." But a few days later they raided another house of praying believers and found the same girl in attendance. Sergei couldn't believe it and, in his anger, beat the girl himself.

Back at the police station he looked over the names of the Christians and continued to struggle with the increasing numbers of young people, especially this one girl, Natasha, who he was sure would have learned her lesson. As Sergei investigated Natasha's records, he learned that she, too, had been a member of the Communist Youth League. The question remained, *What has happened to her that has caused her to become a believer in God?* Sergei had to know more about her, so he had her brought in for questioning. She was scared but courageously answered all the questions. She conveyed her forgiveness to her oppressors and tried to share her faith in God, but Sergei dismissed her, confident he would never see her again.

But only a week later they raided another home and found Natasha praying with other young believers. As the band of Sergei's angry police advanced on the Christians, Victor stood between the men and Natasha and, waving a club, said, "I'm telling you, don't touch her. No one touches her! She has something we don't have." Sergei motioned for Natasha to escape out a side door, but her faith would never escape his mind.

Sergei wrote, "For one of the few times in my life, I was deeply moved. Natasha *did* have something! She had been beaten horribly. She had been warned and threatened. She had gone through unbelievable suffering, but here she was again. Even tough Victor had been moved and recognized it. She had something we didn't have. I wanted to run after her and ask, 'What is it?' I wanted to talk to her, but she was gone. This heroic Christian girl who had suffered so much at our hands somehow both touched and troubled me very much."

The abnormal, otherworldly kind of love and devotion Natasha exhibited haunted Sergei to the point where he decided to jump ship in the icy waters off the coast of Canada near the Soviet territory. He knew his chances for survival were slim but chose to swim to a place where he might find the freedom and love that he saw in the Christians he persecuted. Miraculously, he made it to Canadian soil and immediately went in search of believers to answer his questions. Sergei Kourdakov not only found Christ but spoke openly and testified to his faith in God throughout Canada during the late sixties.

Sergei writes this in the closing lines of his book:

> And, finally, to Natasha, whom I beat terribly and who was willing to be beaten a third time for her faith, I want to say, Natasha, largely because of you, my life is now changed and I am a fellow Believer in Christ with you. I have a new life before me. God has forgiven me; I hope you can also. Thank you, Natasha, wherever you are. I will never, never forget you!*

Perfect love is mature.
Perfect love is effective.
Perfect love is remarkable.

If there is one more quality to add, it is that perfect love is *unforgettable*. Other-worldly. It is a love that in every sense of the word is "perfect." In fact, when we demonstrate love for our enemies and those who are hard to love, we couldn't be more perfect. It is reasonable and well within you this week to be like your Father in heaven. He put it in you. Flawless, you probably are not. If there is anyone who is perfect in the flawless sense, they are probably not aware of it.

As Jesus tenderly poses these questions to you, what is your response? If you want to believe in this kind of love, step out this week and write that

---

* Sergei Kourdakov, *The Persecutor* (Old Tappan, N.J.: Fleming H. Revell, 1973), 251.

letter of grace, say those words of forgiveness, pray that prayer for someone who is hard to pray for, and as you do—you will resemble God. People will see His eyes and hear His voice and sense His touch through your life.

Questions for Reflection and Study

1. What do you think Jesus *really* meant when He commanded us to "love" our enemies? Can you support your answer with examples from the Bible?

2. Do you agree with the statement in this chapter that perfection has more to do with what we do than with what we don't do? Why, or why not?

3. Is there an offense you could never forgive? If so, what is that offense—and why do you feel it is beyond forgiveness?

4. Would you give your life for someone else? Who? Under what circumstances?

5. What are three specific actions you can begin this week in order to come closer to Jesus' goal of "perfection"?

CHAPTER 4

The Clarity
of the Cave

"What are you doing here?"

The word of the LORD came to him: "What are you doing here, Elijah?"

He replied, "I have been very zealous for the LORD God Almighty. The Israelites have rejected your covenant, broken down your altars, and put your prophets to death with the sword. I am the only one left, and now they are trying to kill me too."

The LORD said, "Go out and stand on the mountain in the presence of the LORD, for the LORD is about to pass by."

Then a great and powerful wind tore the mountains apart and shattered the rocks before the LORD, but the LORD was not in the wind. After the wind there was an earthquake, but the LORD was not in the earthquake. After the earthquake came a fire, but the LORD was not in the fire. And after the fire came a gentle whisper. When Elijah heard it, he pulled his cloak over his face and went out and stood at the mouth of the cave.

Then a voice said to him, "What are you doing here, Elijah?"

He replied, "I have been very zealous for the LORD God Almighty. The Israelites have rejected your covenant, broken down your altars, and put your prophets to death with the sword. I am the only one left, and now they are trying to kill me too."

The LORD said to him, "Go back the way you came, and go to the Desert of Damascus. When you get there, anoint Hazael king over Aram. Also, anoint Jehu son of Nimshi king over Israel, and anoint Elisha son of Shaphat from Abel Meholah to succeed you as prophet. Jehu will put to death any who escape the sword of Hazael, and Elisha will put to death any who escape the sword of Jehu. Yet I reserve seven thousand in Israel—all whose knees have not bowed down to Baal and all whose mouths have not kissed him."

— *1 Kings 19:9–18*

* * * * *

I'm not very good at saying No. Bad things happen when I say Yes, and that bad feeling emerges only after it is too late to say No.

That bad feeling surfaced like a submarine rising from the sea as I walked into the first-grade classroom as a substitute teacher for an entire day. I quickly scanned the room to get my bearings, breathed out a deep breath of stress, and looked over the lesson plans left by the homeroom teacher. The first major activity, penciled in, delivered an ironic blow as it read, "What are you doing here?" Not sure if it was a personal note or an actual activity, I commenced to read on. I was a theology student, not an elementary school teacher, and the question caused me to wonder, *What am I doing here?*

I choked down my feelings of inadequacy and soon discovered the exercise, "What are you doing here?" was actually a fun activity in which students draw an environment and use small cutouts of various animals. The objective is to rotate the different animals against various backdrops to see if they belong. For example, a bird placed under the water in an ocean would cause a bright young mind to ask, "What are you doing here?" The question, at its heart, inquires whether the subject matches its context. The activity was fun. We'll talk about how that day went at another time.

If there ever were a biblical example of a fish out of water or a bird swimming in the sea, it is Elijah cowering with self-pity in a cave. Though some of the questions God asks prompt an answer, other questions foster much-needed reflection that brings about a more teachable disposition. First Kings 16 through 19 catalogs a series of amazing events that portray God's presence and providence. The question God asks comes at the end of the story but—to more fully capture the essence of God's inquiry—we need to start at the beginning. In order to make sense of the question, we need to help Elijah answer it. We need to trace back through his journey and see how he arrived in the cave.

James 5:17 claims that "Elijah was a man just like us." My first response to that is, "Right." The events that make up Elijah's life are so rare in mine that I wonder what Brother James was talking about. Perhaps what James meant was that Elijah did have seasons of great moments, when God was in control, guiding and using him; and then there were valleys of despair and caves of depression. He was on fire with moral courage but keenly sensed loneliness and fear. Maybe James is saying that Elijah was human, and the common experiences of humans are basic, no matter who you are.

Elijah came from Gilead, a wild, desolate country on the east side of the Jordan River. This backwoods region was spackled with dense forest; rigid canyons claimed a little town of Tishbe, where Elijah hailed from. Elijah dressed the part of a backwoods boy wearing "a garment of hair and with a leather belt around his waist" (2 Kings 1:8).

Idolatry had become common in Israel, and Ahab took this perversion to new depths. The Bible describes Ahab as one who "did more evil in the eyes of the LORD than any of those before him" (1 Kings 16:30). Furthermore, what makes Ahab so heinous is not that he did bad things but that he pretended those evil things weren't bad at all. First Kings 16:31 claims that Ahab "considered it trivial" to commit the sins he engaged in during his reign. So Ahab, hungry for wealth and influence, married Jezebel, the daughter of Ethbaal, king of the Sidonians. David Roper describes Jezebel: "This crafty, unscrupulous woman came from a long line of monstrous tyrants. Her father was the cruel and vicious Ethbaal, who murdered his way to the throne of the city-state by assassinating his brothers."*

Jezebel wasn't just a bad woman; she was a missionary of evil. She began her religious tyranny by killing off the prophets of the Lord (1 Kings 18:4). Shrines, temples, and groves devoted to Baal worship littered the landscape of Israel. In places where the presence of God once dwelt, Ahab and Jezebel instilled a cohabitation of pagan idolatry with the true faith of Jehovah. This is what Elijah stood up against. It wasn't that the people

---

* David Roper, *Elijah, A Man Like Us* (Grand Rapids, Mich.: Discovery House Publishers, 1998), 15.

totally abandoned their religion; they did something more dangerous. They mixed the truth about the God of heaven with the practices of Baal worship.

What causes Elijah to stand out on the pages of Scripture is the fact that miracles seem to accompany his work, and he appears so confident in his faith.

He stands up to Ahab and promises the drought: "Now Elijah the Tishbite, from Tishbe in Gilead, said to Ahab, 'As the LORD, the God of Israel, lives, whom I serve, there will be neither dew nor rain in the next few years except at my word' " (1 Kings 17:1).

He is fed by ravens: "He did what the LORD had told him. He went to the Kerith Ravine, east of the Jordan, and stayed there. The ravens brought him bread and meat in the morning and bread and meat in the evening, and he drank from the brook" (1 Kings 17:5, 6).

The widow of Zarapheth miraculously feeds him daily:

> Elijah said to her, "Don't be afraid. Go home and do as you have said. But first make a small cake of bread for me from what you have and bring it to me, and then make something for yourself and your son. . . ."
>
> She went away and did as Elijah had told her. So there was food every day for Elijah and for the woman and her family. For the jar of flour was not used up and the jug of oil did not run dry, in keeping with the word of the LORD spoken by Elijah (1 Kings 17:13–16).

When the widow's son dies, Elijah restores him to life:

> Some time later the son of the woman who owned the house became ill. He grew worse and worse, and finally stopped breathing. . . .
>
> The LORD heard Elijah's cry, and the boy's life returned to him, and he lived. Elijah picked up the child and carried him down from the room into the house. He gave him to his mother and said, "Look, your son is alive!" (1 Kings 17:17–23).

Elijah confronts Ahab again with a do-or-die challenge between God and Baal:

> When he saw Elijah, he said to him, "Is that you, you troubler of Israel?"
>
> "I have not made trouble for Israel," Elijah replied. "But you and your father's family have. You have abandoned the Lord's commands and have followed the Baals. Now summon the people from all over Israel to meet me on Mount Carmel. And bring the four hundred and fifty prophets of Baal and the four hundred prophets of Asherah, who eat at Jezebel's table."
>
> So Ahab sent word throughout all Israel and assembled the prophets on Mount Carmel (1 Kings 18:17–20).

It is important to stack the scenes of Elijah's life together because what most people know about the fiery prophet is his brazen faith that commands the miraculous. Elijah listens, and God speaks. Elijah prays, and there is no rain. Elijah promises, and food appears. Elijah pleads with God, and a dead boy is alive. Elijah calls for a face-off between the gods and God, and the whole countryside shows up for the showdown. The guy is on fire. Unstoppable. Seemingly invincible. For Elijah, the truth is black and white, and his challenge is for everyone to step on one side of the line he so boldly scratches in the sand. Listen to his words to the people of Israel as they gather to see the fireworks: " 'How long will you waver between two opinions? If the LORD is God, follow him; but if Baal is God, follow him.' / But the people said nothing" (1 Kings 18:21).

What does Israel's "no answer" to Elijah's appeal mean?

The word *halt* or *waver* actually means "to limp" or "hobble" as though one had a broken leg. One leg of their faith was healthy (they worshiped the God Jehovah) but the other leg was broken (they also worshiped Baal). This is what led to the showdown at Mount Carmel. It is one or the other, not both! God is clear, " 'You shall have no other gods before me' " (Exodus 20:3). Is it possible that one of the reasons we feel like our walk with God limps is that we are loyal to more than just Him? Not one "saint" came forward during his altar call and, per-haps because of this, he believed that he was the only faithful person in Israel.

Though many acts of courageous faith accompanied Elijah's ministry, none is more famous than what he did at Mount Carmel. Read a few dra-matic clips filled with intense trash-talking and graphic theater:

> Elijah said to the prophets of Baal, "Choose one of the bulls and prepare it first, since there are so many of you. Call on the name of your god, but do not light the fire." So they took the bull given them and prepared it.
>
> Then they called on the name of Baal from morning till noon. "O Baal, answer us!" they shouted. But there was no response; no one answered. And they danced around the altar they had made.
>
> At noon Elijah began to taunt them. "Shout louder!" he said. "Surely he is a god! Perhaps he is deep in thought, or busy, or traveling. Maybe he is sleeping and must be awakened." So they shouted louder and slashed themselves with swords and spears, as was their custom, until their blood flowed. Midday passed, and they continued their frantic prophesying until the time for the evening sacrifice. But there was no response, no one answered, no one paid attention (1 Kings 18:25–29).

Elijah constructs the altar for the Lord and makes sure the setting is prepared for an impossible feat that only the God of heaven could per-form.

> Elijah took twelve stones, one for each of the tribes descended from Jacob, to whom the word of the LORD had come, saying, "Your name shall be Israel." With the stones he built an altar in the name of the LORD, and he dug a trench around it large enough to hold two seahs of seed. He arranged the wood, cut the bull into pieces and laid it on the wood. Then he said to them, "Fill four large jars with water and pour it on the offering and on the wood."
>
> "Do it again," he said, and they did it again.

"Do it a third time," he ordered, and they did it the third time. The water ran down around the altar and even filled the trench.

At the time of sacrifice, the prophet Elijah stepped forward and prayed: "O LORD, God of Abraham, Isaac and Israel, let it be known today that you are God in Israel and that I am your servant and have done all these things at your command. Answer me, O LORD, answer me, so these people will know that you, O LORD, are God, and that you are turning their hearts back again" (1 Kings 18:31–37).

The Bible doesn't record a dramatic pause, nor does it describe the apprehension in the eyes of the witnesses there that day. The sacred pages say nothing of Elijah's facial expressions or his posture as he prayed. The Bible simply states, "Then the fire of the LORD fell and burned up the sacrifice, the wood, the stones and the soil, and also licked up the water in the trench" (1 Kings 18:38).

Is there another individual in history who has the courage and faith of Elijah? But the story is not over. Though Elijah's confidence is what stands out on the mountain, he flees the scene, frightened by the threats of Jezebel. That's right, Elijah runs and hides in a cave, which is where God comes to His cowboy prophet with a question: "What are you doing here?"

This is a side of Elijah we haven't yet seen. Disoriented. Depressed. The cagy prophet journeyed for forty days and forty nights, which if taken literally, gave him ample time to decompress from the magical events on Mount Carmel.

He came to a broom tree, sat down under it and prayed that he might die. "I have had enough, LORD," he said. "Take my life; I am no better than my ancestors." Then he lay down under the tree and fell asleep.

All at once an angel touched him and said, "Get up and eat." He looked around, and there by his head was a cake of bread baked over hot coals, and a jar of water. He ate and drank and then lay down again.

The angel of the LORD came back a second time and touched him and said, "Get up and eat, for the journey is too much for you." So he got up and ate and drank. Strengthened by that food, he traveled forty days and forty nights until he reached Horeb, the mountain of God. There he went into a cave and spent the night.

And the word of the LORD came to him: "What are you doing here, Elijah?" (1 Kings 19:4–9).

When the Lord finally gets Elijah's attention, the voice of God invites the prophet to come out of the cave because God is going to pass by. Wind. Earthquake. Fire. And the Scriptures claim "the LORD was not in it." But the Lord's presence came in "a gentle whisper" (1 Kings 19:12).

And so did the question, "What are you doing here, Elijah?"

God's question is repeated, but Elijah's answer seems like a well-rehearsed resignation laced with a little whine: I " 'have been very zealous for the LORD God Almighty. The Israelites have rejected your covenant, broken down your altars, and put your prophets to death with the sword. I am the only one left, and now they are trying to kill me too' " (1 Kings 19:10).

The analytical side of me says, "How can you, Elijah, the greatest prophet of all, go from unshakable resolve to an attitude of self-pity and surrender?" However, the other side of me breathes a sigh of relief because I'm not the only one who witnesses God's glory one day but goes blind to His guiding ways the morning after.

Nevertheless, it is in the quietness, the silence outside the cave, that God's presence reenters Elijah's world. Perhaps there is more to solitude than we credit. Moses. Abraham. David. Daniel. Even Jesus ducked the crowds and stole away to quiet places to restore His perspective. Ellen White comments on Christ's need for solitude:

As one with us, a sharer in our needs and weaknesses, He was wholly dependent upon God, and in the secret place of prayer He sought divine strength, that He might go forth braced for duty and trial. In a world of sin Jesus endured struggles and torture of soul. In communion with God He could unburden the sorrows that were crushing Him. Here He found comfort and joy.*

Ken Jones writes,

[When I walked into my office,] I noticed something I had never seen before. It was round, about the size of a desert plate, and plugged into the wall, giving out a constant noise. It wasn't a loud noise, just constant. What in the world is that thing? I thought as I stopped to stare. I finally asked the receptionist about it. She said, "It's an ambient noise generator. If it's too quiet in here, we can distinguish the voices in the counseling offices, and we want to protect their privacy. So we bought the noise generator to cover their voices." Her explanation made perfect sense to me, but didn't it have to be louder to mask the conversations, I asked. "No," she said. "The constancy of the sound tricks the ear so that what is being said can't be distinguished."†

The white noise of the world can muffle the voice of God unless we get some quiet. Ellen White observed, "We must individually hear Him speaking to the heart. When every other voice is hushed, and in quietness we wait before Him, the silence of the soul makes more distinct the voice of God."§ If Elijah's experience teaches us anything, it is that God speaks to us in the silence and, if still, we can be made whole again. Jesus chose to steal away. Elijah was driven by his circumstances to the cave. Either way, we come to clarity when we quiet our world and open the ears of our soul.

It is likely that the same kind of renewal and reorientation is available for you when the way is unclear. Even Elijah had the wrong answers to

---

* *The Desire of Ages*, 363.
† Cited in Craig Brian Larson, *750 Engaging Illustrations*, 235.
§ *The Desire of Ages*, 363.

God's question, but he had the right heart. So God reconfigures his sensibilities with new information:

"Go back the way you came, and go to the Desert of Damascus. When you get there, anoint Hazael king over Aram. Also, anoint Jehu son of Nimshi king over Israel, and anoint Elisha son of Shaphat from Abel Meholah to succeed you as prophet. Jehu will put to death any who escape the sword of Hazael, and Elisha will put to death any who escape the sword of Jehu. Yet I reserve seven thousand in Israel—all whose knees have not bowed down to Baal and all whose mouths have not kissed him" (1 Kings 19:15–18).

Notice the way new information brings new energy to help Elijah make his way out of the cave. There are three enduring truths that grow out of this new command that gives Elijah new life.

The first truth is, *get up and go.* When God tells Elijah to "Go back the way you came" the operative word is *go*—get moving. The cave is where we find our will to live and press on, but it comes with action. Jane Kise illustrates the way guidance requires movement when she suggests, "Picture yourself in the driver's seat of a car. No matter how hard you crank the wheels, you can't change the direction it's pointed unless you first put it in gear."* Even when you spiritually stall and don't have a clue how to get yourself back on track, get up and go. Go to church. Go to a friend's house and ask him or her to pray with you. Go for a walk and pray for your neighbors or coworkers. Go to the bookstore and look for something to read. Go on a mission trip. Get up and volunteer. Be in motion, because as we walk with God, we begin to discover the opportunities God has for us.

Second, *do what you can do.* Elijah is charged with specific tasks that he can do. The very mood of God's word turns Elijah from retreat mode to a battle-ready general roaring, "Charge!" The command to anoint Hazael, Jehu, and Elisha assumes a massive regime change that God is calling for.

---

* Jane Kise, *Finding and Following God's Will* (Bloomington, Minn.: Bethany House, 2005), 4.

This is precisely the kind of stuff Elijah was born to do! You can see his wild-eyed cowboy expression return to his face as God calls for a serious shift in leadership. Sometimes we find renewed energy when we simply do what needs to get done and what we know we can do.

Sitting in the airport, I waited for my plane and found a place to sit and open my mail. I had about five minutes to kill, so I opened a card that conveyed warm, genuine words of encouragement. The words could not have come at a better time, and then it dawned on me how much good can be done in just a few minutes. The note written couldn't have taken more than three minutes to write, but what a difference it made in my day. Whenever I travel, I take a stack of cards with me because no matter what happens, I can always write a note. I can always say something to help someone else. No matter where I go, I can always do something.

Finally, *know you are not alone.* John Milton once said, "Loneliness is the first thing which God's eye named not good." Yet, at some level, we humans are always alone. No one can know all our thoughts, fears, or wonderments. But what makes us unique as individuals should not make us prone to isolation. It is amazing how community emerges when one person makes the courageous move to speak out or stand up.

Elijah felt as if he were all alone, but he bravely stepped forward and made his loyalty to God plain. Sometimes, courage begets courage, and it takes a leader to stir up the saints. Even now, there are others who believe what you believe, who are sometimes afraid, yet are inspired by the same hope you are, and just may be waiting for a comrade to stand with.

What are you doing here?

Have you retraced the pivotal moments of your life and marked your journey of faith? Have you witnessed moments of fire but also felt the paralysis of uncertainty? *What are you doing here?* What experiences have brought you to the place where you would read a book like this? Have you been to the cave of solitude and stayed there until the fire, wind, and the shaking passed? Did you hear God's voice urge you to move forward? Did He remind you of His ability to care for you and keep you close?

Elijah's life often seems like a roller-coaster ride through supernatural victory to human despair. It is hard to imagine Elijah's journey mirroring ours. It is possible that we may never experience Mount Carmel or the feeling of being completely alone. But if there is anything to take from Elijah's roller-coaster ride of life, it is that God calls us to listen for His voice, in the fire and in the silence. Elijah's story portrays how God attends to us during times of depression and ultimately finds a way to speak hope and clarity into our lives.

Questions for Reflection and Study

1. What are the five "stories" that have shaped your life? Possible answers: Mission trip. Tragic accident. Pivotal move. Affirming words from someone.
2. Which time in Elijah's life do you most identify with—standing on the top of Mount Carmel, calling Israel to make a decision, or hiding in the cave wishing he could die? Why?
3. Have you ever had to do something you knew was right but that was extremely unpleasant? How did you find the courage to do it? How did you feel afterward? Did the experience teach you anything about yourself?
4. If God were to speak directly to you today as He did to Elijah in the cave, what would He say to you? What would be your response to Him?
5. Do you sometimes feel you are the only one who is standing for what is right? Do you sometimes feel everyone else is standing for what is right—except you?

CHAPTER 5

Unmistakable Rest

"Should not this woman be set free?"

On a Sabbath Jesus was teaching in one of the synagogues, and a woman was there who had been crippled by a spirit for eighteen years. She was bent over and could not straighten up at all. When Jesus saw her, he called her forward and said to her, "Woman, you are set free from your infirmity." Then he put his hands on her, and immediately she straightened up and praised God.

Indignant because Jesus had healed on the Sabbath, the synagogue ruler said to the people, "There are six days for work. So come and be healed on those days, not on the Sabbath."

The Lord answered him, "You hypocrites! Doesn't each of you on the Sabbath untie his ox or donkey from the stall and lead it out to give it water? Then should not this woman, a daughter of Abraham, whom Satan has kept bound for eighteen long years, be set free on the Sabbath day from what bound her?"

— Luke 13:10–16

* * * * *

A recent survey reports that 67 percent of people feel they need a long vacation; 66 percent often feel stressed; 60 percent feel time is crunched; 51 percent want less work; 49 percent feel pressured to succeed; and 48 percent feel overwhelmed.

Maybe you feel a little like Tattoo, the basset hound. Tattoo didn't intend to go for an evening run, but when his owner shut the dog's leash in the car door and took off with Tattoo still outside the vehicle, he had no choice. Motorcycle officer Terry Filbert noticed a passing vehicle with something dragging behind. It was "the basset hound picking [up his feet] and putting them down as fast as he could." The officer chased the car to a stop. Tattoo was rescued, but not before the dog had reached a speed of twenty to twenty-five miles per hour, rolling over several times.

Too many of us end up living like Tattoo, our days marked by picking up one foot and putting down the other as fast as we can. One of the most pressing hungers in the world today is for rest. Consider, for instance, Maria Bruner, whose soul was so starved for rest that even though she was an innocent woman, she welcomed the opportunity for time behind bars.

Bruner's husband is unemployed, so she supports their three young children by cleaning other people's houses. While he wasn't working, her husband still managed to run up almost five thousand dollars in unpaid parking tickets. Mr. Bruner kept the tickets a secret from his wife, but as the owner of the vehicle, she is responsible. Maria can't pay the fine, and unless her husband can come up with the money, she will spend three months behind bars in her town jail of Poing, Germany.

What was Maria's reaction? "I've had enough of scraping a living for the family. . . . As long as I get food and a hot shower every day, I don't mind being sent to jail. I can finally get some rest." Police reported that when they went to arrest Maria, "she seemed really happy to see us . . . and repeatedly thanked us for arresting her." While most people taken into custody hide their heads in shame, Maria "smiled and waved at her bewildered family as she was driven off to jail."*

Maria's fatigue echoes across the globe. One evening, a band of college students were lounging around my house late into the evening when I noticed Janelle starting to nod off. Afraid she would sprain her eyelids by jerking them open in order to force herself to stay awake, I asked why she didn't go home and sleep. She slurred a well-thought-out response, "I'm never resting and awake at the same time."

In some cases, sleep only postpones our exhaustion for a few hours, but as soon as the day begins, the children argue, the bills arrive, the errands

---

* Sunday Times, "Family of the Week," *Times Online,* www.timesonline.co.uk.

need running—our sense of purpose and quest for freedom get squeezed out by a deep hunger for rest.

How long have you been tired?

The woman featured in this chapter spent eighteen years trying to find rest from her infirmity. Her story appears only in Luke's Gospel. He tells us, "On a Sabbath Jesus was teaching in one of the synagogues, and a woman was there who had been crippled by a spirit for eighteen years. She was bent over and could not straighten up at all" (Luke 13:10, 11). Jesus uncorks like a potent bottle of Martinelli's, popping with unchecked disapproval at the senseless, inhumane treatment of a woman crippled for eighteen years. The religious leaders didn't physically attack her, but they committed what could be considered an even more severe act—they dismissed her. They overlooked her—her name, her value, her condition.

She had been crippled, bent over, and broken by this illness for eighteen years. She knew every cobblestone and was intimately familiar with every pothole in town, because that's all she saw. Her eyes were always on the gutters and grime of the streets and never on the tops of the trees or birds flying against the backdrop of the clear blue sky.

For the last eighteen years this woman had stumbled in and out of the synagogue, and never once did unmistakable rest come. Not once was rest ever a part of her Sabbath experience. Those who experience chronic pain or injuries understand the enduring nature of fatigue. Ben, a friend who suffers with arthritis, says, "You get so tired of not being able to function that it drains your will to do anything." Furthermore, even when you feel better, it doesn't always mean you are rested. The word *better* is relative—better than what? When you recover from the stomach flu, better is not throwing up. But not throwing up doesn't mean you have recovered, and many experience a relapse because they feel better but aren't well. The same is true for believers when we are not liberated by Sabbath rest.

The crippled woman longed for healing and freedom, which is why she came to the synagogue on the Sabbath. Perhaps she was sick and tired of being sick and tired. And, according to Jesus, nothing is more appropriate on the Sabbath day than finding rest.

But for the Pharisees, the issue was the meaning and purpose of the

Sabbath. Keep in mind that we have two main reference points for the law of God, which includes the command to keep the Sabbath day holy.

The first is the commandment in Exodus 20:11, which reads: " 'For in six days the LORD made the heavens and the earth, the sea, and all that is in them, but he rested on the seventh day. Therefore the LORD blessed the Sabbath day and made it holy.' " The Sabbath is a time to connect with the Creator.

The other passage, Deuteronomy 5:15, contains the same law, but notice that this text gives a slightly different reason for keeping the Sabbath: " 'Remember that you were slaves in Egypt and that the LORD your God brought you out of there with a mighty hand and an outstretched arm. Therefore the LORD your God has commanded you to observe the Sabbath day.' "

In Exodus, the Sabbath commandment asks us to remember God as our Creator. However, in Deuteronomy, the Lord urges us to keep the Sabbath holy as a memorial of our liberty—our redemption, the moment God set us free. In all the things Jesus felt comfortable doing on Sabbath—whether physically, emotionally, spiritually, or socially—setting people free was high on His list.

Not so for the Pharisees. The religious leaders were "indignant" because Jesus acted in a way they thought broke the Sabbath. " 'There are six days for work,' " they declared. " 'So come and be healed on those days, not on the Sabbath.' "

The Pharisees tried to keep the Hebrew faith true to its roots during seasons of moral, ethical, and intellectual bankruptcy. The Pharisees and scribes truly were the most passionate people of faith and duty to God. In order to preserve the rich beauty of God's law and the history of God's people, they made rules and subsets of rules and tried to capture every scenario that might trip up believers in their walk with God. This behavior, of course, became a deformed catalog of unbelievably tedious rules, especially regarding Sabbath keeping. William Barclay comments:

> The commandment says that there must be no work on the Sabbath. The Scribe immediately asks: "What is work?" Work then is defined under thirty-nine different heads which are called "fathers of work." One of the things which are forbidden is the carrying of a burden. Immediately the scribe asks: "What is a burden?" So in the

Mishnah there is definition after definition of what constitutes a burden—milk enough for a gulp, honey enough to put on a sore, oil enough to anoint the smallest member (which is further defined as the little toe of a child one day old), water enough to rub off an eye-plaster, leather enough to make an amulet, ink enough to write two letters of the alphabet, coarse sand enough to cover a plasterer's trowel, reed enough to make a pen, a pebble big enough to throw at a bird, anything which weighs as much as two dried figs.*

These rules were set up so people wouldn't have to think. But the last thing God wants is for us not to think. The last thing God wants is for us to not think about Him. According to the scribes, you could spit on a rock but not on the ground because adding moisture to the soil would make the earth more likely to grow something—it would be farming. Clearly, the institution of rest on the Sabbath had become bigger than the people who were supposed to experience the rest the Sabbath offered.

In Mark 2:28 Jesus said, " 'The Sabbath was made for man, not man for the Sabbath.' " Whatever you do on the Sabbath must have a few qualifying characteristics. The seventh day was to be holy, special, and separate from all the other days (see Genesis 2:2, 3). The Sabbath must cause you to connect with the One who created you, so you always remember who God is and who you are—a child made in His image (see Exodus 20:8–11; Genesis 1:26, 27). As sin drove a wedge between God and His people, the Sabbath was to be a celebration of freedom and a time of reflection on the significance of salvation (see Deuteronomy 5:12–15). Finally, the Sabbath was meant to be a unique marker, a sign that signified relationship to God (see Ezekiel 20:12, 20). Thus, the Sabbath is a time to "save life" and to "do good" (Luke 6:9).

Perhaps it is important to note that the sermon in the synagogue that Sabbath did not bring this woman rest. The special music and prayers of the people did not liberate her. All the building projects and master plans left her exhausted. All the elements of church life were not getting the job done. Therefore, Christ, the Creator and Redeemer, deliberately healed

---

* William Barclay, *The Mind of Jesus*, 152, 153.

this woman, not only to free her but to stir up the minds of the gathered people about the purpose of Sabbath.

The passion pouring out of Christ conveys two things. First, calling the president of the synagogue and anyone siding with him a "hypocrite" is a rebuke loaded with evidence. It was part of the tradition of the Jews to treat beasts of burden with kindness; hence, setting an animal free and leading it to water was well within the boundaries of Sabbath keeping. Being nice to animals is not hypocritical. Being nice to animals and mean to people is hypocritical. The word *hypocrite* means "a pretender," an "actor." To be aware of the needs of a donkey and indifferent to the pain of a child of God is sin.

Second, Jesus notices the woman and reminds everyone that she is, in fact, a daughter of Abraham. That she has been under the bondage of the evil one is offensive to the Savior, which is why He passionately throws out this question to the religious leaders: " 'Doesn't each of you on the Sabbath untie his ox or donkey from the stall and lead it out to give it water? Then should not this woman, a daughter of Abraham, whom Satan has kept bound for eighteen long years, be set free on the Sabbath day from what bound her?' " (Luke 13:15, 16).

There are two unmistakable realities about Sabbath rest. First, if you don't enter into the rest of Sabbath, you will forget who God is. A story is told of a man who was taken away from his family to a prison camp. His children were young, and he knew they would forget him over time. He risked his life to get letters written and messages sent to his children. When other prisoners would strive to buy cigarettes or obtain food and alcohol, he would use his resources to buy pen and paper and to pay a courier to take the letters home. In his letters he poured out his entire soul to his wife and children. Upon his release, some twenty years later, he returned to his village and wondered whether his children would recognize him. Would they even know of him? Did the letters get through? He found his family's hut, and the instant he called to his wife and children, as soon as they heard his voice, they burst out of the hut to embrace the father they knew only through the letters that had made it home. When we forget who the Creator is, we lose sight of who we are.

Second, if you don't enter the rest of Sabbath, you will forget who you are. God knew we would make work our sole identity and reason for living if left to our own devices. We will define ourselves and others around us by what we do, instead of whom we belong to.

God commanded His children to remember Him. He didn't suggest it, allude to it, wish for it, or hope for us to remember Him. He commanded us to remember Him. He knew His children would forget and starve their hearts to death by stuffing themselves with the idea that their purpose in life is to make something out of themselves.

Melba Beal was one of nine black teenage girls chosen to integrate Central High in 1957. In the book *Warriors Don't Cry,* she begins by telling the story that has become what I would call a Sabbath for her. This became an event that stood as a constant reminder of who she was and what made her truly significant.

When she was born, the doctor had to use forceps that injured her scalp and resulted in a serious infection a few days later. Melba's mother took her to the white hospital, which reluctantly took care of the families of the black men who worked on the railroad. In order to save her life, the doctor surgically placed a drainage system beneath her scalp, but her condition did not get better. Her mother tried to get the doctors and nurses to examine the baby girl, but they wouldn't take her seriously. They brushed her off saying, "Just give it time." After a couple of days, Melba's temperature hit 106 degrees, and the little baby began to convulse. So, the family called the minister and family to gather for last rites.

At the hospital Melba's grandmother was rocking her back and forth, singing to her while her mother paced nervously around the room. A black janitor sweeping in the hallway inquired why she was crying, and she explained that her baby was dying because they couldn't stop the infection in her head. The old janitor extended his condolences and made a comment about how the Epsom salts hadn't worked as prescribed. Melba's mother ran after him and asked him what he meant by "Epsom salts."

Melba tells the story:

> He explained that a couple of days before, he had been cleaning the operating room as they had finished up with the surgery. He heard the doctor tell the white nurse to irrigate my head with Epsom salts and warm water every two or three hours, or I wouldn't make it.

Mother shouted the words "Epsom salts and water" as she raced down the hall desperately searching for a nurse. The woman was indignant, saying, yes, come to think of it, the doctor had said something about Epsom salts. "But we don't coddle your kind," she growled. Mother didn't talk back to the nurse. Instead, she sent for Epsom salts and began the treatment right away. Within two days, I was remarkably better. The minister went home, and the sisters from the church abandoned their death watch, declaring they had witnessed a miracle.*

So, fifteen years later, when Melba Beal was selected to integrate Central High, she reflected on the way God had spared her life and equipped her to carry the banner for her people. Knowing who she was became an anchor for what she would become.

Perhaps today you need a reminder of who God is and who you are in Christ. The question Christ asked the people that day He asks on your behalf today, "Doesn't this child of Abraham deserve the freedom that comes from real Sabbath rest?" Maybe, the ultimate message of Sabbath is timelier today than ever before.

Questions for Reflection and Study

1. If you could make one change in your life to slow down its frantic pace, what would it be? How difficult would it be to make that change?
2. Which do you find more appealing—the physical rest or the mental/spiritual rest afforded by the Sabbath?
3. "Rules are necessary in order to protect the sanctity of the Sabbath and the blessings to be found in Sabbath keeping." Do you agree with this statement? Why, or why not?
4. Why do you think Jesus didn't avoid stirring up controversy with the religious leaders by waiting until Sunday to heal this woman?
5. Is it possible that what might be appropriate Sabbath keeping for one person could be inappropriate for another person? Explain your answer.

---

* Melba Beal, *Warriors Don't Cry* (New York: Washington Square Press, 1995), 5.

Chapter 6

Extraordinary Grace in Ordinary People

"What is in your hand?"

Moses answered, "What if they do not believe me or listen to me and say, 'The Lord did not appear to you'?"

Then the Lord said to him, "What is that in your hand?"

"A staff," he replied.

The Lord said, "Throw it on the ground."

Moses threw it on the ground and it became a snake, and he ran from it. Then the Lord said to him, "Reach out your hand and take it by the tail." So Moses reached out and took hold of the snake and it turned back into a staff in his hand.

— Exodus 4:1–4

* * * * *

If you catalog someone's life with enough detail and regularity, you will have a rich variety of good and bad, ordinary and extraordinary. As we look at the questions that God asks, we become mindful of His heart. God questions Adam and Eve because He wants to save them. When Jesus stood up for the sinful woman in the temple courts, He asked a question that would seal her confidence in God's grace. When the Lord peppered the disciples with a thought-provoking sequence of questions about loving our enemies, we see His unimaginable mercy. And, as we learned with Elijah, the clarity comes as we get up and go, obeying His voice. As God's questions permeate our hearts and minds, we are drawn to Him, and the way to go ahead is made clear.

From the aqua bassinet to his exclusion from the Promised Land, Moses lived a most extraordinary life. Even Hollywood was challenged to capture his life accurately and completely. But if Elijah is the sensational prophet of Israel, Moses is the anchor. For centuries, Moses served as the reference point for leadership and devotion. Moses was "the lawgiver." And the Savior, who one day would come and ultimately deliver Israel, is referred to as a prophet like Moses. But the storied journey of Moses takes a pivotal turn when the faithful shepherd turns into a key agent for the redemption of Israel.

This encounter between Moses and God needs a little context. Exodus shows us Moses, born in Egypt and almost a casualty of a paranoid pharaoh (see Exodus 1:8–20); Moses was saved in a basket and adopted by Pharaoh's daughter (see Exodus 2:1–10); Moses defended a countryman and was forced to flee (see Exodus 2:11–15); Moses was making a living as a shepherd (see Exodus 2:15–22); and Moses was encountering God in the burning bush (see Exodus 3; 4).

The question God asks Moses at the burning bush is actually the answer to a question Moses had asked God. Have you ever had someone answer your questions with a question? I would ask my teacher, "What are we supposed to do with this assignment?" And she would answer with a question of her own, "Have you read the instructions?" Sure enough, the answer to my question would be found in my answer to her question! Without fail, one of my favorite professors would answer any inquiries with, "What do you think?" The assumption hidden deep within that annoying response is that learning is an interplay between thinking and responding, listening and sharing.

For example, a mother coaches her young daughter down the water slide, "Come down the slide, honey," the mother urges.

"Is the water deep?" she asks.

"The water is perfect, and you can stand up and touch the bottom. Come on down."

"Will I get water up my nose?" the little girl cries out, hoping to be rescued from the challenge before her.

Mom replies, "Jenny, would I let you go down the slide if it were unsafe?"

"No," she whimpers. Then she closes her eyes and lets go.

The exchange between God and Moses is ironically similar. God says to Moses through the burning bush, " 'Now, go. I am sending you to Pharaoh to bring my people the Israelites out of Egypt' " (Exodus 3:10). But Moses responds to God's command with a question: " 'Who am I, that I should go to Pharaoh and bring the Israelites out of Egypt?' " (verse 11). God says, " 'I will be with you' " (verse 12). Normally, those five words, spoken by God, would be enough. But Moses has more questions for God: " 'Suppose I go to the Israelites and say to them, "The God of your fathers has sent me to you," and they ask me, "What is his name?" Then what shall I tell them?' " (verse 13). Patiently, God replies, " 'I AM WHO I AM. Say to the Israelites: "I AM has sent me to you" ' " (verse 14).

Now, if I'm Moses, that answer, as majestic as it might sound, doesn't cause me to hurry back to Egypt. Moses has just been asked to do something no one on earth has ever had to do. His question is a reasonable one. He asks, " 'What if they do not believe me or listen to me and say, "The LORD did not appear to you" ? ' " (Exodus 4:1).

Douglas J. Rumford observed, "One of the most discouraging misconceptions about following the Lord is that we are usually called to do what we don't want to do with gifts we don't have."* But although Moses may have doubted his qualifications, the mission God called him to was near and dear to his own heart. During his forty years in Pharaoh's court Moses' heart had yearned for the deliverance of his people. Ellen White explains: "His thoughts often turned upon the abject condition of his people, and he visited his brethren in their servitude, and encouraged them with the assurance that God would work for their deliverance."†

But now, in spite of the thought that Moses had given to the deliverance of his fellow Israelites, the challenge God thrusts upon him prompts the humble shepherd to examine all contingencies. Moses is thinking ahead, maybe too far ahead, because the Lord is finished answering his questions. In fact, the God of heaven now has a question of His own.

---

* Douglas J. Rumford, *Questions God Asks, Questions Satan Asks* (Carol Stream, Ill.: Tyndale House, 1998), 100.

† Ellen G. White, *Patriarchs and Prophets* (Mountain View, Calif.: Pacific Press® Publishing Association, 1958), 246.

"Then the LORD said to him, 'What is that in your hand?' " (Exodus 4:2).

I love doughnuts, and I don't buy just one. I buy a dozen, one for each of the three family members—and I eat what's left! I caught my son, Cameron, leaving the kitchen with a fresh, golden, glazed doughnut in his hand, and I asked a ridiculous question. "Cameron, what do you have in your hand?" He just looked at me quizzically and answered slowly in a patronizing tone, completely bankrupt of respect, "Dude, this . . . is . . . a . . . doughnut. A . . . delicious . . . pastry." When you think about it, my question wasn't really a question at all.

"Moses, what is in your hand?"

"A staff."

A simple shepherd's stick, a staff. As common to a shepherd as a cell phone is to a human today. When God turned the stick into a snake and the snake back into a stick, the message finds its mark. There is no need to overstate God's point.

"Moses, it's not about you."

According to Paul, God's "power is made perfect in weakness" (2 Corinthians 12:9). Moses' humility is endearing, but Ellen White points out the danger of continually questioning God:

> These excuses at first proceeded from humility and diffidence; but after the Lord had promised to remove all difficulties, and to give him final success, then any further shrinking back and complaining of his unfitness showed distrust of God. It implied a fear that God was unable to qualify him for the great work to which He had called him, or that He had made a mistake in the selection of the man.*

The stick-and-the-snake lesson conveyed a truth often overlooked by believers: God wants to do extraordinary acts of grace through the ordinary lives of His people. Stick or snake, it doesn't matter. God can turn whatever we have in our hand to His purpose, if we will trust and obey.

---

* *Patriarchs and Prophets*, 254.

When God asked Moses to throw down his staff, the request had two functions. First, God was asking Moses to release his hold on what made him feel secure. And second, He was asking Moses to reach out and grasp His will with faith, even if it was scary. In following this request, Moses—and we—overcomes self-reliance and embraces depending solely on God. Now you can see why God finds it much easier to work with the humility of Moses than the self-assurance of another.

Ronald Pinkerton tells about a hang gliding incident that taught him about humility. As his glider was descending, a blast of air sent him darting toward the ground:

> I was falling at an alarming rate. Trapped in an airborne riptide, I was going to crash! Then I saw him—a red-tailed hawk. He was six feet off my right wingtip, fighting the same gust I was. . . . I looked down: three hundred feet from the ground and still falling. The trees below seemed like menacing pikes. I looked at the hawk again. Suddenly he banked and flew straight downwind. Downwind! If the right air is anywhere, it's upwind! The hawk was committing suicide.
>
> Two hundred feet. From nowhere the thought entered my mind: *Follow the hawk.* It went against everything I knew about flying. But now all my knowledge was useless. I was at the mercy of the wind. I followed the hawk.
>
> One hundred feet. Suddenly the hawk gained altitude. For a split second I seemed to be suspended motionless in space. Then a warm surge of air started pushing the glider upward. I was stunned. Nothing I knew as a pilot could explain this phenomenon. But it was true. I was rising.*

Pinkerton discovered what Moses and many others have learned over the centuries: there is a place where our understanding ends and a greater wisdom begins. God often allows ordinary people to lead so there will be no mistaking the real source of deliverance. We find examples of this

---

* Ronald Pinkerton, *Guideposts*, September 1988.

throughout the Bible. At the Red Sea there is no imaginable way to credit anyone else but God. David kills Goliath; there is no rational way David has a chance unless God is with him. The altar on Mount Carmel is saturated in water, and there can be no other explanation than God alone. The fiery furnace is heated seven times hotter, which presumably will consume a person seven times faster, unless the Son of God is with you in that furnace. And when Jesus sent Peter to fish at the absolute worst time, worst place, and with no human hope to catch even a rubber boot, the result showed that God had to be with him. God is the Master of delivering extraordinary grace through ordinary means.

After all, the Lord says to Moses, " 'Who gave man his mouth? Who makes him deaf or mute? Who gives him sight or makes him blind? Is it not I, the LORD?' " (Exodus 4:11). Then how do we respond to God's question, What is in your hand?

A Portuguese sailing ship ran out of water off the coast of South America. Many days went by, and the crew and passengers were suffering terribly when a second ship appeared on the horizon. The Portuguese ship was able to send a message describing its predicament and asking for help. The reply came back: "Lower your buckets." They didn't realize they were floating at the mouth of the Amazon, where all the water is fresh, even miles out at sea.

Sometimes we resist God's call, because there seem to be some natural obstacles that get in the way. Bruce Larson mentions three roadblocks that get in the way of following God's call to us. One is "we believe we are trapped by our circumstances." Whether it is by our choices or the choices of others that affect us, we seize up and struggle to believe that God can really use us now. A second roadblock is that "we doubt our dreams." Reality is what is possible, and fantasy is what we can only imagine. This is dwarfed thinking, and it shrivels our willingness even to be available for God's purposes. Lastly, "we rely on our instincts." Again, David listened to God's voice, not his instincts, when he chased down Goliath. Gideon beat back his instincts in order to let God's voice be heard in his heart. Our instincts will tell us to always play it safe. I just don't see that in the abundant lives of believers in Scripture.*

---

* Bruce Larson, *What God Wants to Know* (New York: HarperCollins, 1994), 39.

So, what do you have in your hand? Each person today has at least three things in his or her hand.

The first thing we hold is *the "staff of attention."* Throughout the Gospels, Jesus is noted to have *seen* people. In Matthew 9:36, He "saw the crowds . . . [and] had compassion on them." In Matthew 8:14, "He saw Peter's mother-in-law" as He visited their house. In John 9:1, Jesus "saw a man blind from birth." In Luke 17:14, Jesus saw ten lepers who called to Him at a distance. In Luke 7, Jesus meets the widow of Nain during the funeral, and the Bible says, "When the Lord saw her, his heart went out to her" (verse 13). Luke tells us that Jesus "saw through their duplicity" (Luke 20:23), meaning that sometimes you avoid trouble by paying attention.

I went to a Twila Paris concert, and I watched her pay attention to people. After the concert, people came to her, one by one, and whoever sat before her had her undivided attention. I could tell she was genuinely interested in each person as that person poured out his heart and prayed with her. By watching Twila Paris, I truly learned (the hard way) how important it is to be genuinely interested in others.

When I was in my final year of college, I made my way to class passing by a young lady wearing a pink ski coat. I casually extended the greeting, "Hey, how ya doin'?" without even looking at her. I was just being polite. Such a greeting isn't meant to open up the channels of communication so people can connect. It is what we say when we feel too awkward to just walk by someone without saying anything. In this instance, I would have made a better impression if I had just kept my mouth shut. She replied coolly, "What do you care, anyway?" Imagine that! Her response was just plain rude.

I kept walking toward my class, and with each step the weight of my indifference began to constrict my conscience like a giant python. Thoughts of guilt and fraud were pecking at me like vicious birds. I'm trying to use as many animal metaphors as I can to convey my shame—what kind of an insincere animal was I? By the time I reached the classroom door, I could not enter. I turned around and went looking for the girl in the pink coat so I could apologize. I searched everywhere. Two hours later I found her sitting alone in the cafeteria. So I plopped my tray down in front of her and didn't say a word. She looked at me and said what many say when they see me, "Oh no! It's you."

My first words were an apology. "I'm really sorry. I had no intention of even caring about how your day was going. I realize that's wrong. I hope you can forgive me for being so insensitive. I didn't care then, but I do now. What's wrong?"

Her response could have gone either way. The direct approach I chose is not always the best, but the Spirit was working, and she visibly moved from defensive to broken. "My parents just told me that they are getting a divorce," she admitted, "and everything just keeps going on around me while my whole world has fallen apart. And I know it's not true—but no one seems to care."

I did all that I could do. I listened.

Throughout the course of each day we can pay attention to the world that whirls around us. Deliberately keeping our eyes open is an exercise in and of itself, but a worthwhile discipline.

"What is that in your hand?"

Second, we hold *the "staff of experience."* Leo Tolstoy once said, "It is by those who have suffered that the world has been advanced." Perhaps what he meant was that experiences have a unique way of making us particularly useful.

I once was asked to speak to a group of students about the miraculous, but I have had very little experience with miracles. Throughout the Bible there are acts of divine interposition, and part of what makes them amazing is the fact that the events are hard to explain—hence, supernatural. But I know young people who have buried their brothers and sisters, parents who have laid to rest children, and grandparents who stand at the graveside and believe in the hope of the resurrection. I stand in wonder with my hands in my pockets and my heart in my throat because there is nothing I can say or do to explain the miracle of a believer. For this reason we need to recognize that our experience, our struggles, and our pain are, in fact, a staff of help and hope for someone else.

In 1 John 1:1, the aged apostle writes, "That which was from the beginning, which we have heard, which we have seen with our eyes, which we have looked at and our hands have touched—this we proclaim concerning the Word of life."

Cindy bit her lip and choked back the anger she felt because she never wanted to talk about her journey as a cancer survivor. But she knows how her experience can help someone else because when she was in the hospital for chemo, a young woman named Gina came to visit her faithfully. Gina was a nurse, but when she came to spend time with Cindy she pulled the privacy curtain closed and took off her wig, revealing the smooth round head of someone intimately familiar with cancer treatment. Gina spent countless hours with Cindy because it helps to be with people who know from experience what you are going through. So, Cindy regularly made her way as often as she could to the cancer ward and, even though it was hard, she knew it helped both the patients and her.

Not only does our experience with adversity make our lives effective for the cause of grace, but our victories contribute as well.

"What is that in your hand?"

Third, and last, we hold *the "staff of our effort."* Paul, at the end of his letter to the Galatians, punctuated his final words to the church saying, "Let us not become weary in doing good, for at the proper time we will reap a harvest if we do not give up" (Galatians 6:9). It is easy to get tired of helping and giving and sharing. But one staff we all have in our hand today is effort. Whether it be in word or deed, with muscle or just with a smile, we seize an exodus moment whenever we give our effort to someone in need.

My friend Andy is always driving through fast-food windows and coffee shops and paying for the person behind him and speeding off to remain undiscovered. I asked him why he does this, and he admitted, "As a counselor, so much of my work never gets done, but when I make the effort to help someone's day just a little bit, I feel like I've completed something worthwhile. And that feels good."

Sitting in an airport waiting for my plane to board, I noticed a very tired woman with two small children about three and five years of age. The five-year-old was racing around the walkway causing people to stop and dodge the active child. The kid was oblivious to the inconvenience he was causing. In his own world, he continued to buzz around while people shook their heads at the mother's lack of control.

Meanwhile the three-year-old wrestled around on her lap, reaching for a soda cup to get another drink. In the process of drinking, the cup collapsed, and the dark liquid splashed all over both mother and child, as well as a few other well-dressed people nearby. At that point, the mother lost her temper and swatted the little kid on the backside, shouting, "Can't you drink anything without spilling it?"

People began to shake their heads in disgust at such a poor display of parenting. A woman sitting next to me went from being disgusted at the commotion to becoming belligerent. She stomped away and called security. Two men in uniforms came and began talking to the woman; an airline ticket agent joined them. The woman who had reported the incident dropped down in a seat and stated to no one in particular, "Someone had to do something for those children." Just then I watched an amazing thing happen.

A woman in a business suit put down her briefcase and joined the discussion. By this time all eyes were on the little group, and everyone was waiting to see what would happen. The frazzled mother explained her plight to the security officers and the airline agent as they smiled compassionately and nodded with concern. The businesswoman, opening her briefcase, pulled out paper and pens and began drawing pictures of animals and showing them to the three-year-old. He started naming each animal out loud—"pig," "cow," "horsey," "dog." I leaned a bit closer to better understand what was happening, but by that time the plane started to board. A look of relief swept over the mother's face as the security officers and the gate agent helped her gather up her bags and get on the plane. I overheard the businesswoman say, "She's raising those children alone. They've been awake for thirty-two hours. The airline lost their luggage and their baby stroller. Every flight on her way back home has either been delayed or canceled. And her ATM card won't work for some reason."

I don't know who that businesswoman was, but to me, she looked a lot like Moses. Moses was willing to make the effort, to use his staff—or whatever God placed in his hand—for the cause of grace.

"What is that in your hand?"

If you choose to answer this question today, don't take too long—it's a rhetorical question. More important than the answer is the spirit in which you answer, "God, whatever I have, and whatever I can be for the cause of Your grace and for the work of Your glory, I'm willing."

Questions for Reflection and Study

1. What do you feel is the most effective ability that God has given you? What are you doing with it?

2. Does God usually call a person to do something that pushes that person out of his or her comfort zone in order to bring about growth? Or does God usually call us to do those things that we are comfortable with because He has given us the gifts to do them well? Explain your answer.

3. Have you ever resisted doing something you felt God wanted you to do? What excuses did you offer? What was the outcome?

4. In responding to God's leading, how do we determine where the boundary between "faith" and "presumption" is located?

5. What could you do to make a difference in someone's life today? What is preventing you from doing so?

CHAPTER 7

The Lord Speaks

"Where were you when the heavens were made?"

Then the LORD answered Job out of the storm. He said:
"Who is this that darkens my counsel with words without knowledge?
Brace yourself like a man; I will question you, and you shall answer me.
Where were you when I laid the earth's foundation? Tell me, if you understand."

— Job 38:1–4

* * * *

Tearing ligaments in my knee hurt. Missing classes in college almost ended in academic disaster. Limping and hobbling around campus in the rolling hills of Tennessee offered its fair share of ups and downs. But nothing shook my world like watching the video of my knee surgery. The blood didn't bother me; in fact, the scope was so close I could hardly make out what I was watching. What did shock me to the core, however, was the audio. What I heard going on while I had been sleeping deeply disturbed me. Doctors and nurses casually conversed about everything from the chicken salad at the cafeteria to the Atlanta Braves winning the pennant—*while repairing my knee!* I knew this because every once in a while there would be a brief commentary involving my knee ("There's a bone chip." Or, "It's only partially torn."). But the conversation would soon return to lengthy discourse about key vacation spots or someone's dog.

"Are you kidding me?" I shouted as I first viewed the tape. "My knee surgery is only a few commercials interrupting a whole miniseries of drama surrounding the lives of the operating room staff!"

Knowing what goes on behind the scenes can often be TMI—too much information. When my descriptions become too descriptive, my son, Cameron, always interrupts and holds up his hand saying, "TMI—too much information."

I hang around a lot of teenagers who don't eat at the fast-food restaurants where they work. When I ask why, they say, "You don't want to know." But curiosity wins out over discretion, so I prod them further, which is a bad idea because then they tell me in graphic detail what I thought I wanted to know. TMI!

If there is a story in Scripture that offers too much information, it is the story of Job. The behind-the-scenes information rattles our foundations and creates more questions than it answers. Satan and God speak to each other! Satan knows us and thinks certain things about us! God knows us and believes things about us. As a result, a deal is struck, and a test begins.

The whole time Job stands firm, defends God, accepts personal responsibility for his situation as a sinner, while God and Satan watch the drama from the bleachers. TMI. I don't want to know this! Do you?

Some things you just don't want to know. I took my youth group on a camping trip, but the rain did not let up the whole day prior; so, when I arrived in the parking lot, eight teenage boys were waiting to go. Each young man stood in the rain with his gear, some bouncing around with transparent enthusiasm, while the others stood suspiciously still and straight-faced. I'm not a prophet nor the son of a prophet, but for the first time in my life I felt certain I could foretell the future—and it didn't look good. When we arrived at the campsite, the first task was to set up tents and start a fire. The rain stopped, and the cool air began to sink in, so I started looking for wood to build a fire.

Now, men take fire-building personally, almost as a mark of manhood. The elements openly challenged my manhood and won. Of course, everyone on this trip had one thing in common—testosterone. So, everyone began to participate in getting the fire underway. As the boys were making their suggestions, there was a sudden odd moment of silence around the circle, but I failed to look around and see what caused the pause. Then a peculiar thing happened. Everyone in the group agreed that someone needed to go in search of dry wood in the forest. It sounded like a sensible suggestion, and being the only sensible person in the group (and the only adult as well), I volunteered to search for dry wood. Not five minutes into the woods, I heard, *"Boom!"* I dropped my only piece of dry wood and raced through the semidarkness toward the campsite.

As I approached, it looked as if dawn were approaching; the glorious light of a massive bonfire gracing the horizon. I decided not to freak out, so I quietly commented, "That's a nice little fire," looking at the billowing blaze before me. A few chuckles leaked out around the inferno. I just looked at each person quizzically, but none of them would look me in the eye—so, I let it go. As the fire calmed down a bit, one student came to my side and handed me a cup of very hot cocoa but said nothing. I started to ask, "How did...?"

He interrupted, "Trust me, you don't want to know."

Do you really want to know the whole story between God, Satan, and Job? Think of what this story does to some of the clichés that keep us comfortably numb. The platitudes get blown away by the information conveyed in Job's story.

Pain is the reality and result of living in a sinful world. Clearly, this is true on many levels, but some feel pain others inflict, that they don't deserve. We are susceptible to random injustices because we belong to a sinful human race. But in this story, suffering becomes a means to prove God's point that Satan is wrong. That may be right, but it feels wrong.

Sometimes bad things happen because of our choices. Job was faithful. The greatest man in the east. Blameless and upright. What did Job do to merit this experience? Are you telling me that because God knew Job had the character and the faith to handle this experience, He chose Job?

Suffering and persecution build character. This is true. So does discipline, good choices, and a positive, obedient life. You don't need to lose your children or become disowned and diseased to walk intimately with God.

Everything happens for a reason; it's part of God's plan. God's plan is His to reveal, not mine to describe. But when people start talking about what God plans and what God thinks, they enter a danger zone of ignorance.

My thoughts are not God's thoughts, and my ways are not His ways. Some things we know because He told us, but there is a whole universe of things that we don't know. Besides, this exchange between God and Satan feels a little random and somewhat improvised.

As we examine the questions God asks Job, we need to briefly review Job's journey and ultimately what he said to set God off on four chapters of rhetorical questions. The story begins with God and Satan discussing Job. Job's life becomes a stage to view the true measure of his faith in God and the legitimacy of God's relationship with people. Job's wealth, family, and health are removed. His "friends" do their part by explaining to him the meaning and purpose of his predicament. They're sure all this is Job's fault. Even Job's wife joins in for a jab.

Although Job wrestles with his circumstances, he maintains, " 'Though he [God] slay me, yet will I hope in him; / I will surely defend my ways to his face' " (Job 13:15). But over time Job comes to believe that his sin and God's judgment are crushing him; in his self-loathing, he wants to die and get the whole thing over with.

Ten percent of the book of Job is story. Almost 80 percent is about what various people presume about God, His actions, and inaction. The final 10 percent of the book is questions God asks Job.

So let's look at the questions God asked Job. You can scan them briefly in chapters 38–41, but chances are you will need to stop and rest—more for Job's sake than your own. The inquiry starts with God saying,

> "Who is this that darkens my counsel with words without knowledge? Brace yourself like a man; I will question you, and you shall answer me. Where were you when I laid the earth's foundation? Tell me, if you understand. Who marked off its dimensions? Surely you know! Who stretched a measuring line across it? On what were its footings set, or who laid its cornerstone while the morning stars sang together and all the angels shouted for joy?" (Job 38:2–7).

The answer is obvious but not complete, because God continues to ask Job similar questions, all of which make a single point—Job is not God.

In fact, all of these questions have nothing to do with Job, Satan, or Job's friends—or even the behemoth! The questions all declare with universal clarity who God is and what He is like. Douglas J. Rumford explains:

> Never once does God speak of Satan, nor of Job's guilt or innocence, nor of the misunderstanding of Job's friends. God never tells Job why he suffers. Job is not given information concerning his circumstances. Instead, he is given a revelation of God's character.*

God simply fires one question after another at Job, and if there were ever a query that could be considered a no-brainer, you can pick your fair share from some of the following samples:

> "What is the way to the abode of light? And where does darkness reside? Can you take them to their places? Do you know the paths to their dwellings? Surely you know, for you were already born! You have lived so many years!" (Job 38:19–21).

> "Can you bind the beautiful Pleiades? Can you loose the cords of Orion? Can you bring forth the constellations in their seasons or lead out the Bear with its cubs? Do you know the laws of the heavens? Can you set up God's dominion over the earth? Can you raise your voice to the clouds and cover yourself with a flood of water? Do you send the lightning bolts on their way? Do they report to you, 'Here we are'? Who endowed the heart with wisdom or gave understanding to the mind?" (Job 38:31–36).

The answers to the quiz are easy. Just mark one of five multiple choice responses: "I don't know." "I have no idea." "I was not born yet." "God alone." "Um, what is a behemoth?" or "All of the above."

As Job takes this little quiz, it's clear He isn't scoring very well. In fact, he doesn't score at all. But he gets the message. God has never been afraid of questions, but sometimes our questions about the way He works and

---

* Douglas J. Rumford, *Questions God Asks, Questions Satan Asks,* 67.

why He does what He does are nonsensical. C. S. Lewis captured this truth in *A Grief Observed*:

> Can a mortal ask questions which God finds unanswerable? Quite easily, I should think. Nonsense questions are unanswerable. How many hours are there in a mile? Is yellow square or round? Probably half the questions we ask—half our great theological and metaphysical problems—are like that.*

Perhaps it is OK to ask questions of God, but we'll know more if we let Him question us. During times of hardship we ask "Why?" because we want an explanation. It is not that knowing "Why?" will help us manage the pain or better negotiate our way through tragedy. The questions God has for Job force him to look at who God *is* instead of why God does what He does. There is no way on earth we can comprehend the complexities of this life, but we can learn to trust the One who understands it all. At the end of all the questions God asks Job, two things change about Job.

First, Job becomes aware of the massive difference between what he knows and what he doesn't know.

> Then Job replied to the LORD: "I know that you can do all things; no plan of yours can be thwarted. You asked, 'Who is this that obscures my counsel without knowledge?' Surely I spoke of things I did not understand, things too wonderful for me to know" (Job 42:1–3).

The essence of the great controversy has to do with our perceptions of God. Satan's ultimate purpose is to misdirect what we think we know about God and to cause us to become suspicious about what we don't know. The snake said to Eve, " 'Did God really say, "You must not eat from any tree in the garden"?' " (Genesis 3:1). " 'You will not surely die,' the serpent said to the woman" (verse 4). In other words, "God is lying to you." And Satan's final untruth: " 'God knows that when you eat of it your eyes will

---

* C. S. Lewis, *A Grief Observed* (New York: Bantam Books, 1961), 80, 81.

be opened, and you will be like God, knowing good and evil' " (verse 5).

If Satan can twist what you think about God, He can make it hard for you to love Him. Furthermore, if he can tempt you to become suspicious of what you don't know about God, he can make it impossible for you to completely trust your Creator. Perception is everything.

A woman purchased a bag of miniature cookies and sat down to wait for her plane. She rested her belongings in the empty seat next to her. On the other side of the empty seat sat a man reading the paper and sipping a cup of coffee. He smiled at her and continued reading. She opened up the bag of cookies that was on the seat and begin eating a few. She was visibly shocked and slightly embarrassed when the man next to her had the audacity to reach into her cookie bag and begin eating some of the cookies as well. She didn't want to make a scene, but she thought to herself, *This rude man is eating my cookies!*

He continued to eat a few at a time, and as the bag began to empty she grabbed several for herself, the whole time wondering, *How can a person be so clueless of common social graces?* As the man reached for the last cookie, she grabbed the bag and took the last one for herself. The man smiled politely, sipped his coffee, and read his paper until the plane began to board. Sitting in her seat, the woman still couldn't get over the audacity of the cookie thief, until she opened her purse to get a pen and saw her unopened bag of cookies—still in her purse!

Like this woman, Job becomes aware that his perceptions and reality are sometimes not the same thing.

There is a second change in Job, the most important one. What is unmistakable at the end of this drama is the way Job binds himself to the Almighty with loving and loyal trust. Job declares, " 'My ears had heard of you / but now my eyes have seen you' " (Job 42:5). Job experiences God in a new way. Before, his devotion may have been described as mechanical, but now it is emotional.

Before, when Job tried to explain God's behavior, his words might have sounded plausible but not believable. But when you negotiate with God through tragedy and experience personally who He is, what you say about Him is real. Ralph Waldo Emerson claimed, "All I have seen teaches me to trust the Creator for all I have not seen."

Perhaps Horatio Spafford can speak with authority about trusting God no matter what happens. Spafford wrote the words to the famous hymn "It Is Well With My Soul."

> When peace, like a river, attendeth my way,
> When sorrows like sea billows roll—
> Whatever my lot, Thou hast taught me to say,
> It is well, it is well with my soul.

The song may be familiar, but the story behind the hymn deepens the meaning of its message.

The year had been filled with tragedy when Horatio Spafford, a forty-three-year-old Chicago businessman, penned this hymn. He and his wife were still grieving over the death of their son when the great Chicago fire struck and caused them financial disaster. He realized that his family needed to get away, so that fall he decided to take his wife and four daughters to England. His wife and daughters went ahead on the SS *Ville du Havre;* he planned to follow in a few days. But on the Atlantic the *Ville du Havre* was struck by another ship and sank within twelve minutes. More than two hundred lives were lost, including the Spaffords' four daughters. When the survivors were brought to shore at Cardiff, Wales, Mrs. Spafford cabled her husband with the words "Saved alone."

He booked passage on the next ship. It was while crossing the Atlantic that Spafford penned the words to this hymn: "When sorrows like sea billows roll . . . it is well with my soul."*

> When peace, like a river, attendeth my way,
> When sorrows like sea billows roll—
> Whatever my lot, Thou hast taught me to say,
> It is well, it is well with my soul.

---

* William J. Petersen and Ardythe Petersen, *The Complete Book of Hymns* (Carol Stream, Ill.: Tyndale House, 2006), 303, 304.

Though Satan should buffet, though trials should come,
Let this blest assurance control,
That Christ hath regarded my helpless estate,
And hath shed His own blood for my soul.

My sin—O the bliss of the glorious thought!
My sin—not in part, but the whole,
Is nailed to His cross and I bear it no more;
Praise the Lord, praise the Lord, O my soul!

And, Lord, haste the day when the faith shall be sight,
The clouds be rolled back as a scroll,
The trump shall resound, and the Lord shall descend;
"Even so,"—it is well with my soul.

Perhaps the best way to conclude this chapter is with a prayer: *God, we stand with Job before You with so little understanding but with so much love. You have won us with Your care and have awed us with Your majesty, and we trust You—perhaps not without flaws or questions or doubts—but like Job we cling to You in our blindness because our longest night is only a moment in time, and Your beautiful plan cannot be thwarted. Our hope is solely in You. Amen.*

Questions for Reflection and Study

1. Do you agree with the statement, "Suffering and persecution build character"? Why, or why not?

2. Do you agree with the statement, "Everything happens for a reason; it's part of God's plan"? Why, or why not?

3. Try to put yourself in Job's place. How would you have felt: (a) about yourself? (b) about God? (c) about your friends?

4. How do our perceptions of God affect the way we view the things that happen to us in life?

5. Why do some people respond to tragedy with greater faith in God and others respond by losing their faith in Him?

CHAPTER 8

Speed Bumps

"Where is your brother?"

Adam lay with his wife Eve, and she became pregnant and gave birth to Cain. She said, "With the help of the Lord I have brought forth a man." Later she gave birth to his brother Abel.

Now Abel kept flocks, and Cain worked the soil. In the course of time Cain brought some of the fruits of the soil as an offering to the Lord. But Abel brought fat portions from some of the firstborn of his flock. The Lord looked with favor on Abel and his offering, but on Cain and his offering he did not look with favor. So Cain was very angry, and his face was downcast.

Then the Lord said to Cain, "Why are you angry? Why is your face downcast? If you do what is right, will you not be accepted? But if you do not do what is right, sin is crouching at your door; it desires to have you, but you must master it."

Now Cain said to his brother Abel, "Let's go out to the field." And while they were in the field, Cain attacked his brother Abel and killed him.

Then the Lord said to Cain, "Where is your brother Abel?"

"I don't know," he replied. "Am I my brother's keeper?"

The Lord said, "What have you done? Listen! Your brother's blood cries out to me from the ground."

— Genesis 4:1–10

* * * * *

The hike *almost* ended without drama or injury. Leading a group of

85

ten-year-olds was nerve wracking. The last leg of the journey was a down-hill path to a grassy meadow in the park. I watched as the band of junior-age hikers made their way down the trail, and then I noticed something that caused me to start worrying.

Naturally, the kids couldn't just walk down the hill. One had to lurch forward and jog, which inspired the others to do the same. I cautioned them as they picked up speed, but with a rush of adrenaline and a sem-blance of bodily control, the young lads rumbled down the hill. There came a point on the trail, however, where their speed picked up drastically, and I could see the excitement on their faces turn to fear as their momen-tum overtook them. Their shoes smacked the ground with flat sounding slaps as their arms flailed wildly in the air for balance. One at a time they fell at the bottom of the hill as their feet hit the thick sand at the edge of the grass. The bruises and scrapes marked them prominently as their par-ents arrived to take them home!

After each of the parents had communicated their disapproval of my leadership, I looked back at the trail to see if I could tell where they might have avoided their disaster. "Where did they go wrong? Where did their walk get out of control?"

The same questions could have been asked of Cain. Where do you think Cain went wrong? If you compare Cain's life to a hike down a hill-side, where do you think he started running? Where did he get out of control? At what point could he have stopped? Is it possible that Cain got to a point where the only thing that would have stopped him would have been a hard fall at the bottom?

The story of Cain and Abel is a stark reminder that there are two re-sponses to sin. One response is to deny it or to justify it. The other is to admit the sin and repent of it.

The story of Cain and Abel is set in the beginning of human history. Cain and Abel were born outside the Garden but were aware of the story of the serpent, the Fall, and the plan to restore humanity through the sacrifice of God's Son. It is amazing that with such rich, vivid evidence of God's blessings and the curse of sin, one of Adam and Eve's children would adopt the same attitude as Lucifer did and act out his selfish pride.

This story depicts two types of people who travel two different paths. Though Cain and Abel were raised by the same parents, they held very different attitudes about God and His character. This is where their paths diverged. Abel saw God's mercy in the way the Creator provided for the redemption of the human race, but Cain rebelled against God in his heart. The distinction may not have been obvious until it came time to sacrifice.

The sacrifice of blood was a reminder that God would provide a Redeemer. Abel chose to obey God out of genuine trust in the plan of salvation. Cain refused to embrace God's grace and chose to bring an offering that emphasized his own efforts. He perceived God as being harsh and arbitrary, and rebellion stewed inside him. The wages of sin is death (see Romans 6:23) and everyone has fallen into sin (see Romans 3:23), so everyone must choose between two methods of payment—you can pay yourself, or you can let Someone pay for you.

The drama between Cain and Abel is more about the struggle between Cain and self. Although Cain was given a chance to turn around, he held tighter to his stubborn pride and stumbled further away from God.

The Bible draws profound warnings about the danger of anger. Job testifies that " 'Resentment kills a fool, / and envy slays the simple' " (Job 5:2). Furthermore, the wise man claims, "A man's own folly ruins his life, / yet his heart rages against the LORD" (Proverbs 19:3). As witnessed by Abel's tragedy, "Bloodthirsty men hate a man of integrity / and seek to kill the upright" (Proverbs 29:10). Maybe the natural course of selfishness blossoms into hatred for others. It stands to reason that if selfishness is the source of sin, then the goal of sin would be the preservation of self and the destruction of others. Conversely, the selfless person begets love for others as a natural course. It seems almost too simplistic, but anger can sneak up on us. Sometimes we do things in anger that feel so right at the time, but afterwards we know are wrong. Speak when you are angry—and you'll make the best speech you'll ever regret.

Perhaps the most frustrating part of the way of Cain is that, like someone running downhill, there seems to be no way to stop. God's questions come to us as they came to Cain, and their purpose is to be something like a speed bump set to slow us down so we don't self-destruct or destroy someone else. Cain runs roughshod over every attempt God makes to save him. Although the story doesn't have a happy ending, we can learn from Cain's mistakes.

There are four speed bumps that guide us away from destruction:

Speed Bump #1—Check your core beliefs. The slightest touch on the rudder can send a ship completely off course. A gentle nudge of the steering wheel may run a car off the road. A gap or crack in the foundation of a house will cause the structure to crumble. In the same way, our bedrock assumptions about God and people determine the ultimate outcome of our lives. Cain's core beliefs about God were skewed from childhood—not by poor parenting but by a flawed perception of God. Cain never walked in the Garden of Eden; he only heard the story and saw the angels guarding the entrance. Perhaps deep within Cain, the belief seethed that God reacted harshly, perhaps unfairly, toward his parents. Ellen White describes the source of Cain's basic distrust of God:

> Cain cherished feelings of rebellion, and murmured against God because of the curse pronounced upon the earth and upon the human race for Adam's sin. He permitted his mind to run in the same channel that led to Satan's fall—indulging the desire for self-exaltation and questioning the divine justice and authority.*

The Bible says, "In the course of time Cain brought some of the fruits of the soil as an offering to the LORD. But Abel brought fat portions from some of the firstborn of his flock" (Genesis 4:3, 4). Whether Cain simply did not understand the significance of the sacrifice or his pride repelled the notion that the wages of sin is death, his offering conveyed his core belief. Cain's sacrifice failed to recognize sin and the need for redemption. When Cain brought his groceries, he essentially said, "This is what *I* can do." Sacrifice has to do with life and death, not red or green peppers. But this tendency did not come from Cain's father, for Adam fully understood and embraced the plan of salvation:

---

* *Patriarchs and Prophets*, 71.

To Adam, the offering of the first sacrifice was a most painful ceremony. His hand must be raised to take life, which only God could give. It was the first time he had ever witnessed death, and he knew that had he been obedient to God, there would have been no death of man or beast. As he slew the innocent victim, he trembled at the thought that his sin must shed the blood of the spotless Lamb of God. This scene gave him a deeper and more vivid sense of the greatness of his transgression, which nothing but the death of God's dear Son could expiate. And he marveled at the infinite goodness that would give such a ransom to save the guilty.*

Cain simply couldn't stomach the means by which God chose to save humanity from the Fall—his core beliefs were broken. When we fail to accept the basic truth that selfishness and sin end in death, as an immovable rule, other options become viable.

A farmer was teaching his son to plow straight rows in the field. "Choose a mark to focus on that will guide your line, and follow it," the father instructed.

The boy found an object and plowed the field. But when the father observed his work, he was astounded by the way the rows all weaved back and forth. "Didn't you understand my instructions? What happened?"

"I did exactly what you said," the boy replied, "but the cow I used to mark my line kept moving."

The unchangeable law of life and death is nonnegotiable, and neither is salvation. There are two ways to pay for sin: your death, or Someone pays for you through His death. This is the basic message of the sacrifice.

As Cain sought to appease God with a gift basket instead of blood, the Bible declares, "The LORD looked with favor on Abel and his offering, but on Cain and his offering he did not look with favor. So Cain was very angry, and his face was downcast" (Genesis 4:4, 5). Herein lies an attribute about God that many overlook. Some perceive the Lord as one who watches and waits for us to mess up—and then pounds us with judgment. That's not the God of Scripture. God watches, but He warns. God intervenes and

---

* *Patriarchs and Prophets,* 68.

interrupts our lives with occasional speed bumps. However, only the sacrifice of His Son will break our fall.

Speed bumps seem like a nuisance, but speed kills. Because God deeply loved Cain, He tried to slow down Cain's momentum before he lost control. So God asked Cain a series of speed-bump questions: " 'Why are you angry? Why is your face downcast? If you do what is right, will you not be accepted? But if you do not do what is right, sin is crouching at your door; it desires to have you, but you must master it' " (Genesis 4:6, 7).

God pleaded with Cain to slow down and think about where his misguided mind was taking him. God offered Cain a way out, which brings us to our second speed bump.

Speed Bump #2—Don't ignore the problem. Paul advises, " 'In your anger do not sin': Do not let the sun go down while you are still angry, and do not give the devil a foothold" (Ephesians 4:26, 27). Rock climbers know about footholds. Two qualities about footholds are important. First, the smallest, most subtle protrusion can be a foothold, and second, a foothold can support a tremendous amount of weight.

In *A View From the Zoo,* a former zookeeper has this to say:

> Raccoons go through a glandular change at about twenty-four months. After that they often attack their owners. Since a thirty-pound raccoon can be equal to a one-hundred-pound dog in a scrap, I felt compelled to speak of the change coming to a pet raccoon owned by a young friend of mine, Julie. She listened politely as I explained the coming danger. I'll never forget her answer. "It will be different for me . . . ." And she smiled as she added, "Bandit wouldn't hurt me. He just wouldn't."
>
> Three months later Julie underwent plastic surgery for facial lacerations sustained when her adult raccoon attacked her for no apparent reason.*

---

* Cited in Roy Zuck, *The Speaker's Quote Book: Over 4500 Illustrations and Quotations for All Occasions* (Wooster, Ohio: Kregel Academic and Professional, 1997), 352.

Sin comes packaged in a seemingly harmless disguise. Cain had covered his disrespect for God with an outward attempt to worship, but deep within, a problem grew even though God offered him a way to deal with his problem. Can you think of times in your life when you needed to stop a course of action or thought process? You sensed the warning but ignored the danger. Thomas Fuller once said, "A fault denied is twice committed."

Furthermore, we tend to ignore sin because it seems so harmless from the viewpoint of our intentions compared to its consequences. And so the momentum of sin propelled Cain faster and harder toward ruin. Cain held tightly to his core beliefs about God and ignored the warnings given by his Creator. Just as you feel it is humanly impossible to stop when you are running downhill—and give in to the momentum—so it can be with sin. But, by the grace of God, it is not impossible to stop running faster and faster into sin.

Speed Bump #3—When you feel like you can't stop, try crashing. Just prior to Peter's betrayal, Christ spoke these words to him: " 'Simon, Simon! Indeed, Satan has asked for you, that he may sift you as wheat. But I have prayed for you, that your faith should not fail; and when you have returned to Me, strengthen your brethren' " (Luke 22:31, 32, NKJV). Even when your propensity for sin is great, Jesus believes the best about you. Sinners have stopped short of disaster before.

Highways with steep grades often have a runaway truck ramp. Basically, these ramps are a safe way to stop when brakes fail. In August 2002, a woman was driving with her dog over Teton Pass in Wyoming when she experienced car trouble. She called a wrecker, and when the tow truck driver arrived, she and her dog climbed into the cab of the truck. As they started down the mountain, her bad situation turned worse. The brakes on the tow truck failed! A skilled driver, he maneuvered the speeding truck through the turns, but he became so focused on trying to negotiate the curves that he didn't even notice the signs for runaway truck ramps. In order to use the ramp you have to make a split-second choice to commit to that lane. But the truck driver froze, and they crashed. The woman and dog survived; the driver didn't.

Sometimes, when we're out of control, we think we might be able to stop or avoid disaster. Yet, the best thing to do is to crash. By crash, I mean to admit you're in trouble and deliberately force yourself toward help, even though it may hurt.

Skiers and snowboarders do it all the time. On the slopes, I've found myself completely out of control heading for trees and, although falling would be uncomfortable (mostly to my pride), the trees would prove to be much more unpleasant. Cain should have taken the runaway truck ramp. He should have fallen to the ground to avoid the trees.

Instead, in a premeditated fury, Cain consummated his hatred toward God by killing his own brother. While God asked many questions to check Cain, hoping to steer him toward a better way, the force of his destruction was too strong. "Where is your brother?" God asked.

The stone-cold son of Adam bounces over the speed bump and casually replies with another question, "Am I my brother's keeper?" Clearly, Cain was out of control, and the propulsion of his hatred pulled him away from repentance.

Speed Bump #4—Repent or die. The word *repent* means to "change your mind" so much so that you change the direction you are going. Although Cain chose not to repent, he was not irrevocably bound to his course. God has proven to be far more patient than any human. But patience doesn't always lead to repentance. Sadly, Jude refers to "the way of Cain" (verse 11) as a stubborn refusal to embrace God's grace and turn away from selfish pride. Complete repentance is the only way to finally avoid the end of anger—death.

Barry Marshall and Robin Warren are two doctors who have studied ulcers. While many try to treat ulcers with antacids and pain relievers, these doctors have discovered that most ulcers are really the work of bacteria called *Helicobacter pylori*. Daniel Haney observes, "It turns out that about half of all U.S. adults are infected with *H. pylor*. . . . Most don't get ulcers. But when ulcers do occur, the bug is probably responsible for 80 percent or more."* Of course, many try to treat the symptoms but aren't aware there is a cure for the source of the problem—antibiotics.

---

* Daniel Haney, "The Ulcer Bug," *Daily Herald,* April 8, 1996, Suburban Living.

God's question calls us to stop and check the sin stirring within us. For some of us, there is sin at the early stage of core beliefs. There may be no visual evidence of rebellion, but we are filled with beliefs that are incongruent with God's kingdom.

For some, sin has reached the danger zone, and God inquires, "Why are you angry? Why is your face downcast? If you do what is right, will you not be accepted?"

He urges us to accept the grace that can save us, if we stop and turn to Him. Or perhaps, we are so deeply enmeshed in a life of disobedience to God that there seems to be no hope. But there *always* is a way—if we have the will to respond.

These two brothers represent two ways to deal with the problem of sin. Cain trusted self. Abel trusted in the sacrifice that pointed forward to Christ.

It's our choice.

Questions for Reflection and Study

1. Given that they had the same upbringing, how do you explain the fact that Cain and Abel ended up so different in their attitudes toward God?

2. Where do you think Cain first went wrong? What might he have done to change course?

3. Is it the sacrifice we bring or the act of sacrificing that is more important to God? What does the story of Cain suggest?

4. In what way do our sacrifices (those things we do in response to God) reflect our ideas about Him?

5. Do you think Cain set out to disobey God by bringing the fruits of his garden as a sacrifice? Can we bring the correct sacrifice and still not be worshiping properly? Explain your answer.

CHAPTER 9

Appreciation Is Not Gratitude

"Where are the other nine?"

On his way to Jerusalem, Jesus traveled along the border between Samaria and Galilee. As he was going into a village, ten men who had leprosy met him. They stood at a distance and called out in a loud voice, "Jesus, Master, have pity on us!"

When he saw them, he said, "Go, show yourselves to the priests." And as they went, they were cleansed.

One of them, when he saw he was healed, came back, praising God in a loud voice. He threw himself at Jesus' feet and thanked him—and he was a Samaritan.

Jesus asked, "Were not all ten cleansed? Where are the other nine? Was no one found to return and give praise to God except this foreigner?" Then he said to him, "Rise and go; your faith has made you well."

— Luke 17:11–19

* * * * *

On a September evening in 1860, the steamer *Lady Elgin*, bearing about three hundred passengers, left Chicago in the face of a threatening storm, bound for Milwaukee. About two-thirty the next morning, the schooner *Augusta* collided with the *Lady Elgin*. The captain of the *Lady Elgin* assessed the damage and decided to proceed without asking for assistance. But within an hour, the ship began to fall apart, and the passengers found themselves in the waters of Lake Michigan, clinging to the wreckage and trying to reach the shore.

A number of the survivors managed to get close to land, but the undertow of the waves breaking on the shore carried them back into the lake, and many drowned. Only about thirty persons came to shore alive, and of these, seventeen were saved by a single young man, Edward W. Spencer, a student at Northwestern University.

Spencer was a seminary student at Garrett Theological Seminary and awoke to the sound of students reporting a shipwreck not far from their campus. He was a strong, competent swimmer. He dove into the chilly waters of the lake and swam out to rescue one person after another. He had rescued fifteen people and was warming himself by a fire when a cry came that two more survivors had been sighted holding on to some debris from the ship. Fighting back his exhaustion and ignoring the injuries he had sustained so far in his rescue attempts, Edward Spencer went out again and brought these two individuals to shore. Some two hundred people died in the accident; of the ninety-eight who survived, Edward Spencer saved seventeen.

But Spencer never returned to the seminary. His life changed drastically that morning. The injuries he sustained left him paralyzed for life. Later, he was interviewed by a newspaper reporter in California, who asked, "What do you recall about the rescue?"

Spencer replied, "Only this; of the seventeen people I saved, not one of them ever thanked me."

Maybe they didn't have a chance. Perhaps they were too busy telling others about Edward Spencer's heroic behavior. Their lives were saved by the efforts of a man who would never walk again. Did they not appreciate his sacrifice?

There does seem to be a gap between appreciation and gratitude. Appreciation is more a matter of common courtesy, a respectful vote of affirmation. But gratitude erupts from the soul. The source of gratitude is heartfelt and genuine, almost unstoppable. Appreciation can be an afterthought; gratitude is a preoccupation.

My sons, Morgan and Cameron, are typical kids; they love gifts. But what I admire about both of them is their sincere gratitude for what they receive.

At the height of his popularity, Mark Twain could command five dollars per word for his writing. When this became known, someone wrote him saying, "Dear Mr. Twain, enclosed is five dollars. Please send me your best word." Mark Twain sent a one-word reply: "Thanks."

Jesus healed ten men of leprosy, but only one returned to give thanks. In this book we've been looking at questions God asks us. These questions give us a window into God's heart, a doorway into His will for our lives. Answering God's questions is perhaps more critical than any question we might ask of Him. In the stories we have looked at so far, it's clear whom God is questioning.

But not in this story. Jesus inquires, " 'Were not all ten cleansed? Where are the other nine? Was no one found to return and give praise to God except this foreigner?' " (Luke 17:17, 18). Is Jesus directing this question to the one leper who did return? Is He looking curiously at His disciples for an explanation? Or is He just asking a general question out loud—directing it to no one in particular?

Before we answer Jesus' question personally, we need to unpack this story with its rich insights into what Jesus is really asking.

Consider a few key points:

Leprosy. No other disease in Scripture seems to portray the work of sin like leprosy. In fact, the term *walking death* captures the common perception of the disease. When people were diagnosed with leprosy, they were excommunicated from society. In some cases their names were taken off the public records of living citizens, for it was only a matter of time before they died. But leprosy attacks the central nervous system first before it ever affects the skin. Jerry Vines graphically captures the way leprosy destroys a person:

> For no reason he would have a feeling of fatigue. Then his joints would begin to get sore. One day he would notice little white spots all over his skin. Later those white spots would begin to harden into nodules. They would turn from white to pink to brown, and then become scaly. The appearance of his face would change until he began to resemble a lion. The nodules would ulcerate all over his body, producing a foul odor. They would cover his vocal chords so that when he breathed there would be a wheezing sound. When he talked his voice would be raspy. His eyebrows would fall out. His

hair would turn white. Inch by inch this man's body would begin to rot. As he walked he would have putrid spots where the pus oozed out of his feet. His fingers and toes would begin to fall off.*

It is one thing to have someone call you unclean, but an entirely different level of hopelessness comes when you are forced to yell "unclean" regarding yourself. Some records indicate that lepers were not to get within fifty yards of healthy people in the open air.

It's interesting that the one of the ten who comes to Jesus is a Samaritan. The Jews and the Samaritans were bitterly prejudiced against each other. The Jewish religious leaders even called Jesus a "Samaritan" as an insult (see John 8:48). There was no love lost between the two groups. But the ten are together. It is uncanny how tragedy can bring humanity together. In the death-lock of their leprosy, these men had forgotten they were supposed to hate each other and knew only that they were in need.

He saw them. We often avoid seeing people we don't want to think about. As you pull off the exit, there is a man and a woman holding a sign asking for food or money. A dozen reasons flood your mind why you should ignore them: *My kids are in the car; I can't stop. I'm not really sure what these people would do with money I might give.* Any number of red flags can surface, and so you look the other way, change the radio station, or simply become preoccupied with something other than the people outside your window.

But Jesus saw these lepers. David writes, "The LORD is close to the brokenhearted / and saves those who are crushed in spirit" (Psalm 34:18). Jesus not only saw them but responded to their plea for help. Perhaps they had heard Jesus handled cases of leprosy. Even if He wouldn't—or couldn't—it was worth a try. When you're facing inevitable death, you tend to take more chances and seize as many opportunities as you can.

The ritual of cleansing and the law of the leper. The Bible says, "As they went, they were cleansed" (Luke 17:14). Their healing came the moment they obeyed the command to go see the priest. There were several reasons

---

* Jerry Vines, *Exploring the Gospels: Mark* (Neptune, N.J.: Loizeaux Brothers, 1990), 29.

that a visit to the priests would be their first action as healed individuals. First, in order to be readmitted into society, they must be examined by the priest and pronounced clean. It's not hard to understand why you might be tempted to skip that step, given the elation and relief you would have felt and your desire to see your family again. But at some point you would have to go through the ritual.

I believe, however, that Jesus told them to go and show themselves to the priest for a greater reason than simply to take care of their paperwork. For the leper, the ceremony of cleansing had a deep, enduring spiritual experience embedded in its ritual.

> "These are the regulations for the diseased person at the time of his ceremonial cleansing, when he is brought to the priest: The priest is to go outside the camp and examine him. If the person has been healed of his infectious skin disease, the priest shall order that two live clean birds and some cedar wood, scarlet yarn and hyssop be brought for the one to be cleansed. Then the priest shall order that one of the birds be killed over fresh water in a clay pot. He is then to take the live bird and dip it, together with the cedar wood, the scarlet yarn and the hyssop, into the blood of the bird that was killed over the fresh water. Seven times he shall sprinkle the one to be cleansed of the infectious disease and pronounce him clean. Then he is to release the live bird in the open fields" (Leviticus 14:2–7).

Imagine the scene. A leper comes to the priest, and the priest must perform this ceremony outside the city. Where was Christ crucified? Outside the city. Then the leper watches as two live birds are brought out; one is killed over running water (or as the Hebrew has it, *living water*). The blood of the bird is mixed with the living water and gathered in an earthen vessel. The one who has been healed watches the dead bird and the bowl of blood and water intently. What could such a person be thinking? Why blood? Why a bird—a living creature? What does this mean? The meaning is made clear when the one healed watches as the live bird is dipped in the blood and water and set free over an open field. Picture the man standing there gazing into the sky as the live bird flaps its wings and the blood and water spray off as the bird soars freely. If leprosy portrays sin, then experiencing this ritual becomes very important. It signifies your redemption from the deadly disease of sin. Clearly, this service is about the Savior and the sinner.

No wonder Jesus wanted the healed lepers to see the priest. He knew that if they went through this ritual, the significance of their salvation would be deeply embedded in their hearts and minds. Unforgettable. Genuine gratitude and a life of adoration and worship would result.

At least that was the plan. But instead of getting lost in the significance of their salvation, they got lost in their elation at being healed—all but one.

One returned. The text doesn't say whether this man went to see the priest or not, but it does say, "One of them, when he saw he was healed, came back, praising God in a loud voice. He threw himself at Jesus' feet and thanked him—and he was a Samaritan" (Luke 17:15, 16.) Herein is gratitude, deep devotion, and heartfelt adoration for Christ, the Healer. What is more is that the one who is making all the noise is a Samaritan— Luke makes this point intentionally.

More than the other Gospels, Luke's Gospel contains more stories about outsiders getting in, have-nots having their fill, and the unforgivable receiving mercy. When the single healed leper returns to give thanks, Jesus is prompted to ask a question we all should try to answer—not with words but with action. " 'Were not all ten cleansed?' " Jesus asked. " 'Where are the other nine? Was no one found to return and give praise to God except this foreigner?' " (Luke 17:17, 18).

Have you been cleansed? Have you been set free by Calvary? How do you answer this question actively? Has the cross of Christ become the basis for your living? Is it your reference point for your life? Consider how life became different for the person in this story:

In 1997, the *Chicago Tribune* reported a story about a skydiving accident. Michael Costello, a parachute instructor, jumped out of a plane with Gareth Griffeth, a novice skydiver. Gareth would soon discover how fortunate he was to have such a skilled instructor. When Gareth attempted to open the parachute, it failed, and the two men fell straight toward the ground, locked together. But just before they hit the ground, Michael Costello rolled, hitting the ground first and, thus, broke Gareth's fall. The instructor died instantly, but Gareth survived, fracturing his spine though not to the extent of paralysis.*

How can we respond to Jesus' question? Do you have rituals and reminders that bring you back to Calvary? Are there songs you sing or pictures you look at that remind you of when the Son of God took your place? The sacrifices of the Old Testament are not just mindless events to keep people religious. They are moments to view, to celebrate, to seal in your heart the amazing grace of God.

Questions for Reflection and Study

1. Who are the "lepers" in our society today? How do most Christians relate to them? How would Jesus relate to them if He were on earth today?

2. Have you ever experienced ingratitude after doing something significant for another? How did you feel? What lessons did you draw from the experience?

3. What could society do today to better serve the "outcasts"? What could the church do? What could the individual Christian do? What could you do?

4. Does the fact that a person may misuse or mismanage the help we provide—money, food, shelter, our time, etc.—excuse us from helping? What practical considerations should enter into our decisions about becoming involved with those who need help?

5. How do you think Jesus felt when only one of the ten healed lepers returned to thank Him? How do you think it affected His attitude toward those needing help?

---

* "Sky Diver Killed Saving a Novice," *Chicago Tribune*, June 25, 1997.

CHAPTER 10

Reality Check

"What are you discussing as you walk along?"

Now that same day two of them were going to a village called Emmaus, about seven miles from Jerusalem. They were talking with each other about everything that had happened. As they talked and discussed these things with each other, Jesus himself came up and walked along with them; but they were kept from recognizing him.

He asked them, "What are you discussing together as you walk along?"

They stood still, their faces downcast. One of them, named Cleopas, asked him, "Are you only a visitor to Jerusalem and do not know the things that have happened there in these days?"

"What things?" he asked.

"About Jesus of Nazareth," they replied. "He was a prophet, powerful in word and deed before God and all the people. The chief priests and our rulers handed him over to be sentenced to death, and they crucified him; but we had hoped that he was the one who was going to redeem Israel. And what is more, it is the third day since all this took place. In addition, some of our women amazed us. They went to the tomb early this morning but didn't find his body. They came and told us that they had seen a vision of angels, who said he was alive. Then some of our companions went to the tomb and found it just as the women had said, but him they did not see."

He said to them, "How foolish you are, and how slow of heart to believe all that the prophets have spoken! Did not the Christ have to suffer these things and then enter his glory?" And beginning with Moses and all the Prophets, he explained to them what was said in all the Scriptures concerning himself.

As they approached the village to which they were going, Jesus acted as if he were going farther. But they urged him strongly, "Stay with us, for it is nearly evening; the day is almost over." So he went in to stay with them.

When he was at the table with them, he took bread, gave thanks, broke it and began to give it to them. Then their eyes were opened and they recognized him, and he disappeared from their sight. They asked each other, "Were not our hearts burning within us while he talked with us on the road and opened the Scriptures to us?"

— Luke 24:13–32

* * * * *

The book *Blink* is about how intuition is often more accurate than our logical thought processes. Malcolm Gladwell tells how an art dealer, Giafranco Becchina, tried to sell a statue for just under ten million dollars. This statue stood tall, and its construction appeared relatively flawless. A museum in California was thinking about acquiring the piece but had to determine whether the work of art bore the marks of a priceless relic or a fraud. All of the documents testified to its authenticity. A geologist from the University of California spent two days examining every inch of the statue with a high-resolution stereo microscope. The scientific analysis, through the use of spectronomy, X-ray defraction, and X-ray fluorescence certified the statue must be old, very old.

The museum agreed to purchase the work of art. But three people, Fredrico Zeri, Evelyn Harrison, and Thomas Hoving, in spite of the scientific evidence, had a gut reaction to the sculpture. Zeri noted that something about the fingernails bothered him. Harrison simply had a sick hunch about the genuineness of the sculpture. And when Hoving saw the statue, he sensed that it looked "fresh," not something you'd say about anything 2,500 years old.

Over time, the documents that verified the age and authenticity of the statue revealed inconsistencies. Finally, the truth emerged; the sculpture had not been preserved for over two thousand years but was a five-year-old forgery.*

---

* Malcolm Gladwell, *Blink* (New York: Little, Brown and Company, 2005), 3–8.

Do you go by your guts or by good data? A case can be made for both—because both have been wrong as well as right. As disciples of Christ, we often walk through seasons of doubt and dismay. When the way isn't clear and the "whys" go unanswered, what do you do? Take a look at what might be the darkest, most confusing hours in the life of Christ's most devoted disciples.

Trying to the put pieces together, two shell-shocked followers of Christ stumbled down the road on a seven-mile trek home. Maybe the disciples replayed all the moments when Jesus stood in complete control of disastrous situations. Charging demoniacs. Empty lunch boxes and well-fed crowds. Fifteen-foot waves and hundred-mile-an-hour winds. Dead people breathing again. Vanishing leprosy. Losers winning. Outsiders belonging. The crowds. The solitude. The sense of purpose shared by all who walked with Christ. Have you ever had a truckload of information but not a clue about how to sort it all out?

Christ came to the two bewildered disciples, who were walking westward, away from Jerusalem. The sun was staring at their faces as it made its way toward the horizon. Jesus joined the travelers, raw with the events of the weekend still in their minds. The sounds, the smells, the horror of the whole experience had placed these disciples into a tailspin where they simply did not know what to think or what to do.

Have you ever been there—on the road to Emmaus? We all have those seasons when life just doesn't seem to add up. Your plans fall apart. The family you thought would be perfect becomes flawed. During these times, do you ever try to just sort it all out logically? In the same way that Christ made His way onto the Emmaus path with the two disciples, He makes His way to us. The question Jesus asked is subtle but poignant. "What are you discussing together as you walk along?" From the text it is hard to know what they were discussing. Maybe they were trying to piece together the events of the last few days. Maybe they were just stumbling along without really talking about them. Whatever it was, the beauty of Jesus' question forces them to talk about what had happened. Why is this question so important? Because walking and talking on the way is the only way.

The way. You know how we name roads after people. Who would have thought a person would be named after a road? It's true! Followers of

Christ were named the Way, which means, "a road or path." Check it out. Acts 9:2; 19:9, 23; 24:14, 22 describe the disciples of Christ as members of *the Way*. In Greek, the words *road* and *way* are the same. The story of the two travelers on the road to Emmaus is an anchor point for people who follow Christ but who sometimes flounder around in a fog of dismay.

I call these reality checks, things to do when the world is screaming one thing in your ears but your stomach is whispering something else. At one time or another, every follower of Christ has been down the Emmaus road, where the truth is not always clear, and your beliefs don't always make sense. A reality check rarely does away with doubt or immediately dispels frustration or fear, but at the end of the road, if you stay on the road, the person of Christ will become clear to you.

There are three reality checks as we travel the Emmaus road.

Reality Check #1: There are times when you think you see clearly when, in fact, you are clearly blind. Don't always believe what you see! Talk about it. Listen. It usually takes time to make sense of complicated situations.

Have you ever noticed that some people are internal processors while others are external processors? Internal processors think through their ideas sequentially and, when they have refined their notions, they speak coherently. Then there are the external processors. These are the people who can think only when their mouths are moving. They often don't make sense, initially. They sometimes contradict themselves. Because they have to hear and speak their thoughts for their thoughts to make sense, they often meander around in their conversations. But they ultimately find their way.

Of these two disciples on the Emmaus road, the Bible says that their "faces [were] downcast" (Luke 24:17). This may have been true literally, but it was also true spiritually. The two could see only the events of the weekend. In a way, they were blinded by their own shortsightedness.

Seeing the big picture as well as the microscopic is important for those who travel the Emmaus road. If these travelers had only tried to zoom out, they might have seen whom they were walking and talking with. The Bible says, "As they talked and discussed these things with each other, Jesus himself came up and walked along with them; but they were kept from recognizing him" (verses 15, 16). It is hard to know whether they didn't recognize Jesus or whether Jesus purposely disguised Himself. Either way, they were unable to see the Truth right in front of them.

Paul says, "We live by faith, not by sight" (2 Corinthians 5:7). What a difference it would have made if they had just widened their scope of vision to include what they believed to be true—walking by faith. Bill Hybels, talking about vision, tells the following story:

> The story is told of two prisoners in one small cell with no light except what came through a tiny window three feet above eye level. Both prisoners spent a great deal of time looking at the window, of course. One of them saw the bars—obvious, ugly, metallic reminders of reality. From day to day he grew increasingly discouraged, bitter, angry, and hopeless. By contrast, the other prisoner looked through the window to the stars beyond. Hope welled up in that prisoner as he began to think of the possibility of starting a new life in freedom. The prisoners were looking at the same window, but one saw bars while the other saw stars. And the difference in their vision made a huge difference in their lives.*

Having seen what happened to Jesus, the wayfarers couldn't see past the bars. We need to admit that, on the journey with Christ, our vision can be tricky. Without fail, we will always be able to trust the Word of God, and our trust in His promises will enable us to endure. With the eyes of faith and the vision of a broader perspective to negotiate through the fog, we will see the promises of God emerge in time.

Reality Check #2: There are times when your information is right but your conclusions miss the mark. Don't close the door on what you know to be true. Some make the mistake of thinking that the truth they know is all there is to know. Notice how each statement the disciples made on the road to Emmaus is correct, but notice how they arrive in despair instead of joy:

---

* Bill Hybels, *Who You Are When No One Is Looking* (Downers Grove, Ill.: InterVarsity Press, 1987), 35.

" 'About Jesus of Nazareth,' " they replied. " 'He was a prophet, powerful in word and deed before God and all the people' " (Luke 24:19).

So true. Although Jesus was more than "just a prophet," their assessment is accurate.

" 'The chief priests and our rulers handed him over to be sentenced to death, and they crucified him; but we had hoped that he was the one who was going to redeem Israel' " (verses 20, 21).

Three times prior to His arrest, Jesus announced this would happen. The entire Old Testament sacrificial system was based on this happening. John the Baptist said, " 'Look, the Lamb of God, who takes away the sin of the world!' " (John 1:29). What did his hearers think that meant? Furthermore, their hopes for the redemption of Israel came true!

" 'And what is more, it is the third day since all this took place' " (Luke 24:21). Didn't Jesus promise that He would rise on the third day?

" 'In addition, some of our women amazed us. They went to the tomb early this morning but didn't find his body. They came and told us that they had seen a vision of angels, who said he was alive. Then some of our companions went to the tomb and found it just as the women had said, but him they did not see' " (verses 22–24).

And why are you staring at the ground stumbling down this road? Everything Jesus said would happen—happened!

The two wayfarers really tried to make complete sense out of the Crucifixion weekend but drew conclusions about Christ's death too soon. Every word they said conveyed fact. But if they had known whom they were walking with, their statements would have led to a different experience.

Reality Check #3: There are some things we experience today that will make sense only later. Don't give up on learning and growing. When the time is right, what you believe, know, and experience will click together in a way that you cannot mistake. "Beginning with Moses and all the Prophets, he explained to them what was said in all the Scriptures concerning himself. . . .

"When he was at the table with them, he took bread, gave thanks, broke it and began to give it to them. Then their eyes were opened and they recognized him, and he disappeared from their sight. They asked each other, 'Were not our hearts burning within us while he talked with us on the road and opened the Scriptures to us?' " (verses 27–32).

All the questions and unresolved ideas came together in the moment they saw Jesus break the bread. They saw Him, and everything began to make sense. *It clicked.*

Have you ever had a dream turn out all wrong and become a nightmare? But then you wake up? For the disciples, this weekend had been like a dream, then a nightmare. Then they woke up to find Jesus standing before them!

Perhaps this story depicts one truth: that even in our most shortsighted, hard-headed, slow-hearted moments, Jesus still walks with us. Know this. There is no backwoods trail so distant or superhighway so treacherous that Jesus won't saunter up beside you and ask, "What's up?" And like everyone else who is on the Way, you, too, will make it through that long walk and find the clarity to run with certainty and joy. So, keep walking.

Questions for Reflection and Study

1. What are some of the ways we can fail to recognize Jesus when He appears to us today?
2. Have you ever faced a major disappointment? How did you find your way through it? What lasting effects has it had on your life?
3. What part do logic and reason play in making sense of life's disappointments? What part do faith and trust play? How do the two connect? Or do they?
4. How can we keep our eyes fastened on the reality of Jesus and His love when everything around us is going to pieces? List four or five specific actions.
5. Why didn't the disciples recall Jesus' predictions about His death and understand better what was happening? What does their experience teach us about ourselves?

CHAPTER 11

Matthew, Mark, Luke, Ed, and John

"Who do you think I am?"

When Jesus came to the region of Caesarea Philippi, he asked his disciples, "Who do people say the Son of Man is?"

They replied, "Some say John the Baptist; others say Elijah; and still others, Jeremiah or one of the prophets."

"But what about you?" he asked. "Who do you say I am?"

Simon Peter answered, "You are the Christ, the Son of the living God."

Jesus replied, "Blessed are you, Simon son of Jonah, for this was not revealed to you by man, but by my Father in heaven. And I tell you that you are Peter, and on this rock I will build my church, and the gates of Hades will not overcome it. I will give you the keys of the kingdom of heaven; whatever you bind on earth will be bound in heaven, and whatever you loose on earth will be loosed in heaven." Then he warned his disciples not to tell anyone that he was the Christ.

— Matthew 16:13–20

* * * * *

Jesus asked many thought-evoking and response-provoking questions. Some questions marinate in your mind and make you wonder. For example: "Someone told him, 'Your mother and brothers are standing outside, wanting to speak to you.'

"He replied to him, 'Who is my mother, and who are my brothers?' " (Matthew 12:47, 48). Other examples of Jesus' insightful questions include,

" 'Why do you break the command of God for the sake of your tradition?' " (Matthew 15:3). " 'What good will it be for a man if he gains the whole world, yet forfeits his soul? Or what can a man give in exchange for his soul?' " (Matthew 16:26). " 'Who of you by worrying can add a single hour to his life?' " (Matthew 6:27).

The nature of a thought-evoking question is that you can ruminate on it, and, like a seed, it might bear the fruit of some action in time. But other questions demand an immediate response, and no question is more pivotal than Jesus' question, "Who do you say I am?"

It's rare to have someone be so vulnerable as to ask, "What do you think of me?" My friends, parents, and wife never ask that question—I assume, because they already know the answer. But the disciples faced some do-or-die challenges. Several times, their Rabbi had already voiced prophecies about His demise. Religious leaders were mounting their efforts to put Jesus to death. People were not responding to their Master with the same kind of openness as before. Overall, there might have been some uncertainty among the disciples about just how to answer Jesus' question.

If you could tell only three stories from the Bible to convey what God is like, what three would you tell? Just preparing your thoughts for an answer causes you to sort and choose those attributes that you think are crucial. So, what would you say if someone were to ask you, "Who is Jesus?" Answers that start with "Um" and "Well" and "It's like, ya know" will not suffice.

You don't want to mess up this answer. Neither did the disciples, so they remained quiet. But Peter answered at last, because he couldn't stand the silence (if he isn't asking questions, then he's answering them). Peter asks more questions than all the other disciples combined.

Peter asked Jesus to unpack and explain some of His hard sayings (see Matthew 15:15; Luke 12:41). Peter inquired how often he needed to forgive others (see Matthew 18:21). Peter wondered out loud about what reward the disciples would get for leaving everything behind (see Matthew 19:27). Peter was the one who asked about the withered fig tree (see Mark 11:21). Peter even asked questions of the risen Christ (see John 21:20–22).

So, when Jesus asks the disciples, " 'Who do you think I am?' " Peter breaks the silence and responds, " 'You are the Christ, the Son of the living God' " (Matthew 16:16).

The Christian movement moves only because people answer that question. It's not enough simply to think about it or to form an opinion about Christ. No, when you answer out loud, you become a witness.

The screeching tires and hollow "woof" of metal crushing metal still haunts my senses every time I drive by the spot. My New Year's Eve plan consisted of a large pizza and a lonely evening unpacking boxes and moving furniture into our new home, while my wife and child visited relatives hours away. The accident occurred when an oncoming car swerved into my lane and smashed my economy-size car head-on, bouncing me deep into juniper bushes. Imagine a kindergartener colliding headlong with a two-hundred-fifty-pound linebacker at top speed. That linebacker was an eighty-nine-year-old woman, attempting a left-hand turn as I inconveniently thwarted her efforts with the front of my car.

The story becomes even more surreal. The little old lady who jousted me off the road with her 1974 Dodge Dart immediately left the scene, on foot, and headed to the bank to make a deposit before the New Year. Unbelievable! After I negotiated my way out of the wreckage, the lights of emergency vehicles emerged and found me, my smashed car, and an empty classic Dodge.

The policeman asked, "Where is the other driver?" When I told him, "I think she went to the bank" he almost administered a sobriety test—on *me*! After a few minutes, the little old lady exited the bank and underwent a thorough examination by the paramedics and the police. Her words almost caused me to come unglued. "I was just turning to go into the bank, and all of a sudden this car crashed into me." Unbelievable!

The officer reinterviewed me because clearly my word meant nothing against the tender demeanor of a sweet eighty-nine-year-old lady. Just as I began to explain what *really* happened, a young man walked over from the emergency vehicles and explained to the policeman, "I saw the accident." His witness, his testimony, saved me.

A witness is somebody who saw or heard something that happened and gives evidence about it. Are you a witness? Have you seen and heard? Are you willing, as a disciple of Christ, to take the witness stand by your words and lifestyle?

Christ commented on Peter's testimony saying, " 'Blessed are you, Simon son of Jonah, for this was not revealed to you by man, but by my Father in heaven. And I tell you that you are Peter, and on this rock I will build my church, and the gates of Hades will not overcome it' " (Matthew 16:17, 18).

First, Jesus removed any opportunity for Peter to get a big head; He did so by pointing out that Peter's confession wasn't something that he had thought up but something that God had revealed to him. Then Jesus affirmed Peter for taking the witness stand and sealed his simple testimony as the basis for building His church.

> For six thousand years, faith has builded upon Christ. For six thousand years the floods and tempests of satanic wrath have beaten upon the Rock of our salvation; but it stands unmoved.
>
> Peter had expressed the truth which is the foundation of the church's faith, and Jesus now honored him as the representative of the whole body of believers.*

Finally, Jesus promised that His followers' continual and faithful witness would stand as an invincible force, even against the threat of death.

Notice the impact of the witness of the woman at the well. After a few moments of theological fencing, she discovered Christ to be the long-awaited Messiah, and she testified, " 'Come, see a man who told me everything I ever did. Could this be the Christ?' " (John 4:29). The result of her witness was that "many of the Samaritans from that town believed in him because of the woman's testimony, 'He told me everything I ever did' " (John 4:39). But the ripple effect of her testimony continued when many others came to meet Christ personally, producing a whole new crop of disciples! Check it out: "Because of his words many more became believers. They said to the woman, 'We no longer believe just because of what you said; now we have heard for ourselves, and we know that this man really is the Savior of the world' " (John 4:41, 42).

---

* *The Desire of Ages*, 413.

It's time to take the witness stand!

When Chris Terry made his way through high school, no one believed he possessed a serious bone in his body. Everything seemed a big joke to him. Then a shift occurred, a shift so real that his life dramatically changed. Chris began to appear regularly at church. He ventured on a few mission trips. He became my son's Sabbath School teacher! Chris experienced a metamorphosis—a transformation so real that those who had known him before wondered, "What happened?"

One afternoon Chris arranged for his class to sing at a retirement village; then and there Chris shared a few words about his journey. I watched and listened as he testified about how Christ had transformed his life. I glanced at his Sabbath School pupils sitting on the front row, fixated on Chris, taking in every word. I watched my son, Cameron, as his eyes followed his teacher's every move. Later that week my son told me he wanted to give his heart to Christ totally.

The power of a personal testimony is unmistakable.

Observe the way the apostle John authenticates his books and letters with the language of a witness: "The man who saw it has given testimony, and his testimony is true. He knows that he tells the truth, and he testifies so that you also may believe" (John 19:35). "This is the disciple who testifies to these things and who wrote them down. We know that his testimony is true" (John 21:24). Not only does John testify, but he explains how bearing witness to who Christ is bears the fruit of fellowship and joy in each other:

> That which was from the beginning, which we have heard, which we have seen with our eyes, which we have looked at and our hands have touched—this we proclaim concerning the Word of life. . . . We proclaim to you what we have seen and heard, so that you also may have fellowship with us. And our fellowship is with the Father and with his Son, Jesus Christ. We write this to make our joy complete (1 John 1:1–4).

As Christian believers answer the question "Who do you say I am?" they expand the kingdom of God and deepen their own sense of ownership in the person of Christ.

Ed, a faithful deacon in a church I served as pastor, frequently used to tell his "eternal life story," as he called it. Everyone heard it—several times. And the way he shared his testimony made it hard to know whether his "eternal" life story meant that he was bearing witness about "eternal life" or that he was simply taking forever to tell his life story!

In his Bible, Ed had inserted fifteen single-spaced pages entitled "Eternal Life Story" between the books of Luke and John. I chided him once about how the book of Revelation gives a stern warning that anyone who adds to this book will receive the plagues. The blood drained from his face as he stared at me in horror.

"Ed, I'm kidding," I said quickly, trying to relieve his panic. I realized he had taken the joke very seriously. While Ed stood in front of me, still pale with worry, I turned the pages of his worn Bible past the book of "Ed" to the book of John and read to him the verses mentioned previously (John 19:35; 21:24; 1 John 1:1–4), assuring him that his "gospel" would not cause him to receive the plagues. I've come to believe that because the legacy of the Christian movement rests on whether we tell who Christ is to us, we should all, like Ed, insert our pages into the sacred story.

A common response I run into is, "I don't have a testimony." What such a person is really saying is that what he or she would say about Christ is either not very well thought out, not dramatic enough to mention, or not complete enough to demonstrate faith in Christ. Here are a few pointers that might help you get started on your very own personal gospel.

Describe your life before you became a disciple of Christ. Sharing what your life was like before you chose to follow Christ is crucial, but some have an easier time at this than others. I often find young people who "grew up with Jesus" and who sometimes feel robbed of a "real" conversion experience. Know—please know—that your journey is crafted by God's hand and the promptings of His Spirit. Some might say, "I have always been a disciple," but I would say, "You may have always been a child of God, but a disciple is someone who *chooses* to follow and learn from Christ." Also, your testimony is not about you as much as it is about what God has done for you. Some testimonies seem more interesting when they track through every detail of a sordid life; and while such turnarounds are interesting, Christ should be the most engaging part of your story.

Paul's "before Christ" experience in Acts 9 is brief, but in Philippians 3:3–6 the great apostle describes his life before he met Christ on the Damascus road. It doesn't sound dramatic, but it is real.

Reflect on and articulate pivotal moments in your journey. Ask yourself, "What events or experiences played a pivotal role in my decision to say Yes to Jesus? What happened that caused me to understand, believe, and receive Jesus into my life?" For the woman at the well it was a "chance" meeting. The demoniacs met Christ in the heat of a supernatural fight. Paul met Christ after being blinded on the road. Philip and Andrew bumped into Jesus after hearing a few inspiring words from John the Baptist. James and John would never forget how their nets filled with fish. Mary would always remember that day when Jesus set her free from seven demons. And throughout eternity, Zacchaeus will replay the scene from the sycamore tree.

Wendy Murray Zoba says that one of the most effective evangelistic tools that Campus Crusade for Christ has developed is the *Jesus* film. She writes,

> Several years ago in Peru, during the insurgence of the Sendero Luminoso (Shining Path), a Wycliffe couple was traveling to show the film in a village. Their vehicle was intercepted by the Senderos, and they feared for their lives (with just cause). Instead of killing them, however, the terrorists decided to seize their equipment, including the film projector. The husband boldly suggested that they might as well take the film reels too. Some time later, a man contacted them to say that he had been among the Senderos who had robbed them. He told them they watched the film seven times (out of sheer boredom), and some had been converted through it. He came to apologize and to tell of his ministry in preaching and evangelism.*

Damien, an acquaintance, shared with me what his life was like prior to an awakening that occurred while he was in high school:

---

* Wendy Murray Zoba, "Bill Bright's Wonderful Plan for the World," *Christianity Today,* July 14, 1997, 24.

I grew up in a Christian home, went to church and sang the songs. I did not go to Christian schools so I always encountered situations that challenged my Christianity. I had a biology teacher that openly mocked religion and caused me to wonder if my faith in Christ was a fake. I prayed, but really never prayed to God personally, just repeating what I was taught. I read the Bible, but not to listen for God's voice but because it seemed like the right thing to do. I wondered to myself, "Why am I a Christian?" So disturbed by the crisis going through my head, I put God to the test and prayed, "God reveal yourself to me." No immediate response came. But a week later I walked through a parking lot on my way to the bus stop and saw my biology teacher leaving the building and walking to his car. His demeanor was different than in class. As I watched him, he just seemed lost and empty. I realized that God was revealing Himself to me by showing me the sadness of my teacher. I thanked God for reminding me of two things: He was with me (as He had always been), and others needed Him.

Think about how your life is different today because of Jesus. Again, be honest and hopeful. Philippians 1:6 promises, "Being confident of this, that he who began a good work in you will carry it on to completion until the day of Christ Jesus." Something happens as you convey your storied journey with Christ. As disciples of Christ, we are marked for life with passion for Christ and a mission to tell His story to others. Bruce Larson tells of his discovery of Christ:

While still a teenager, I served in the army in World War II. But after the war, as part of the occupying forces, I found myself in a moral meltdown. Anything and anyone was for sale for some nylons or a chocolate bar. I hated the corruption and the immorality around me, but I was part of it. I knew that going home, starting college, beginning a career, and getting married would not change me. I'd still be the same weak and sinful person. I was all alone one night, standing guard in a bombed-out factory in Stuttgart, Germany, when things changed dramatically. I was thinking about my life to date and my inability to be the person I wanted to be. I thought about the God I had always believed in, and I put out my cigarette, took my carbine off my shoulder, knelt down, and began to pray: "Jesus, if You really are there, take over my life. I can't promise You I'll change, because I am weak, but I want You to be the Lord of my life." My life from that moment on took a whole new direction, and, even with occasional detours or mishaps along the way, the direction has never changed.*

Think it through and write it out! It may be that God will send someone your way who will need to hear your story about God's work in your life. Be ready to testify! Answer the question, "Who do you say I am?" with the story of your life and make a contribution to what people may think of Christ.

Questions for Reflection and Study

1. Review your life and pick three moments that were key to your conversion and share how those events or experiences shaped your decision for Christ.

2. Would you like to know what your closest friends really think about you? Why, or why not?

3. What would you tell someone who asked you, "Who is Jesus, and what meaning does He have for your life?" How are you different because of Jesus from the way you would be if He were not a part of your life?

4. Is every Christian expected to be a witness? What is involved in witnessing for Jesus?

5. Do you feel you have little or nothing to witness about as a Christian? How do you think your view of your Christian experience would differ from the way a spouse or close friend might see your walk with Jesus?

---

* Bruce Larson, *What God Wants to Know*, 69.

CHAPTER 12

Can, Has Done, Will Do

"Do you believe this?"

Jesus said to her, "I am the resurrection and the life. He who believes in me will live, even though he dies; and whoever lives and believes in me will never die. Do you believe this?"

"Yes, Lord," she told him, "I believe that you are the Christ, the Son of God, who was to come into the world."

— *John 11:25–27*

* * * * *

Of all the questions Jesus ever asked, perhaps none was more carefully set up than the question He asked Martha upon arriving at Lazarus's funeral. Let's examine a few facts before we respond to the big question.

On his arrival, Jesus found that Lazarus had already been in the tomb for four days. Bethany was less than two miles from Jerusalem, and many Jews had come to Martha and Mary to comfort them in the loss of their brother (John 11:17–19).

In Jewish culture it was, as Barclay puts it, "a sacred duty to come to express loving sympathy with the sorrowing friends and relations of one who had died."* In fact, visiting the sick and comforting those who have

---

* William Barclay, *The Gospel of John*, vol. 1 (Philadelphia: Westminster Press, 1975), 90.

lost loved ones are nonnegotiable acts of a faith community, as expected as showing respect during the Pledge of Allegiance or facing the flag during the national anthem. Everyone does it.

"When Martha heard that Jesus was coming, she went out to meet him, but Mary stayed at home" (verse 20). From the biblical evidence, we know that Martha is the mover and shaker of these two sisters, while Mary is the mystic. Martha is a woman of action, while her sister is more reflective. No wonder Martha went to meet Jesus, because she always had something to say about everything. In this case, although she has rehearsed some of her lines, there is one thing she will have to say that may not have been in her script.

" 'Lord,' Martha said to Jesus, 'if you had been here, my brother would not have died. But I know that even now God will give you whatever you ask' " (verses 21, 22). Even as the words came out of her mouth, they were biting. Jesus absorbs the blow, because she is right. He has the power to do something. God is perceived responsible for suffering if He can do something about it. Scripture teaches, however, that God takes personal responsibility by offering the solution to the sin problem. But Martha can't see the big picture. Even as the words came out her mouth, Martha's hopeful fix-it mentality kicked in and tried to appeal to Jesus, even after Lazarus had been dead for several days.

"Jesus said to her, 'Your brother will rise again.'

"Martha answered, 'I know he will rise again in the resurrection at the last day' " (verses 23, 24). The resurrection was a debated concept in Jewish theology. Some sections of Judaism deemphasized or even denied the resurrection or life after death. But, clearly, most Jews in the time of Christ believed there would be a resurrection to life. Throughout the Gospels, Jesus made reference often to the reality of a resurrection.

"Jesus said to her, 'I am the resurrection and the life. He who believes in me will live, even though he dies; and whoever lives and believes in me will never die' " (verse 25). This statement is much bigger than we can comprehend. When Jesus claims to be the Resurrection and the Life— what else is there? There is nothing more to be. Perhaps this is what Paul means when he claims that death will be swallowed up in sweet victory (see 1 Corinthians 15:54). We are talking about a complete reversal of the human psyche. Currently, death has humanity beat. People have tried throughout the modern era to find a way to invent, create, innovate, develop, and defend ourselves against death. Today, we have made it possible to stall death in some cases, but it is only temporary. People tend to fear death because death always wins.

And when Jesus makes this claim to be the Resurrection and the Life, He follows it up with a question that begs a response from everyone who will one day face death. " 'Do you believe this?' " (verse 26). Jesus could have let the notion saturate and simmer a while in Martha's mind, but He didn't. This would be no time for reflection. Jesus knew Martha needed a flag to stick in the ground. Martha needed a line in the sand that she could physically and emotionally step across. We are the same as Martha, because when we face death, whether it involves family, a friend, or our own mortality, we long to do more than think—we crave action. Jesus offered Martha a chance to speak the words of belief that would begin to grow hope in her heart the moment she uttered an answer.

Augustine once said, "What can be hoped for which is not believed?" Before the work of hope moves us courageously forward into whatever dark valley we face, we must first believe. And when we refer to belief, we are not necessarily speaking of the certainty of Paul saying, "I know whom I have believed" (2 Timothy 1:12). Paul made that statement at the height of his moral courage. When we speak of belief, we also include the desperate father begging Jesus to rid his son of an evil spirit. Jesus replies, " 'Everything is possible for him who believes' " (Mark 9:23). But the poor father, transparent as glass, admits, " 'I do believe; help me overcome my unbelief!' " (verse 24). If one can utter words of belief, then— even if mixed with doubt—faith will grow, and courage will follow. Can you answer the question today? If you can say the words, then the impact will be immeasurable.

Colin Chapman, in *The Case for Christianity*, quotes Ugandan bishop Festo Kivengere's account of the 1973 execution by firing squad of three men from his diocese:

> February 10 began as a sad day for us in Kabale. People were commanded to come to the stadium and witness the execution.

Death permeated the atmosphere. A silent crowd of about three thousand was there to watch. I had permission from the authorities to speak to the men before they died, and two of my fellow ministers were with me. They brought the men in a truck and unloaded them. They were handcuffed, and their feet were chained. The firing squad stood at attention.

As we walked into the center of the stadium, I was wondering what to say. How do you give the gospel to doomed men who are probably seething with rage? We approached them from behind, and as they turned to look at us, what a sight! Their faces were all alight with an unmistakable glow and radiance.

Before we could say anything, one of them burst out: "Bishop, thank you for coming! I wanted to tell you. The day I was arrested, in my prison cell, I asked the Lord Jesus to come into my heart. He came in and forgave me all my sins! Heaven is now open, and there is nothing between me and my God! Please tell my wife and children that I am going to be with Jesus. Ask them to accept Him into their lives as I did."

The other two men told similar stories, excitedly raising their hands, which rattled their handcuffs. I felt that what I needed to do was to talk to the soldiers, not to the condemned. So I translated what the men had said into a language the soldiers understood. The military men were standing there with guns cocked and bewilderment on their faces. They were so dumbfounded that they forgot to put the hoods over the men's faces!

The three faced the firing squad standing close together. They looked toward the people and began to wave, handcuffs and all. The people waved back. Then shots were fired, and the three were with Jesus. We stood in front of them, our own hearts throbbing with joy, mingled with tears. It was a day never to be forgotten. Though dead, the men spoke loudly to all of Kigezi District and beyond, so that there was an upsurge of life in Christ, which challenges death and defeats it. The next Sunday, I was preaching to a huge crowd in the hometown of one of the executed men. Again, the feel of death was over the congregation. But when I gave them the testimony of their man, and how he died, there erupted a great song of praise to Jesus! Many turned to the Lord there.*

It was this kind of hope that fanned the Christian movement into a flame, because it's impossible to deny the power of a hope bigger and stronger than death. The Scriptures are filled with the theme that God can, has, and will conquer death.

I happened upon three boys outside a shopping mall. Having just finished Tae Kwon Do class, they were waiting for a ride. I was waiting, as well, so I listened as an argument started. "I can break a board with a side-kick," announced one.

Another chimed in, "That's easy. I can break a board with my fist."

"Well, I can break two boards together with my elbow," bragged the third lad.

The estimates of their prowess continued to escalate until one of them went too far, claiming, "I can break two bricks with my head."

The others stopped, looked intently at him, and said, "Let's go back inside and see you do it."

Seeing he was trapped, he brushed them off, saying, "I can do it; I just don't want to."

One anchor point to hang on to is that not only does God want to conquer death, He can. Without skipping a beat or stuttering, Jesus sent the disciples out to " 'heal the sick, raise the dead, cleanse those who have leprosy, drive out demons' " (Matthew 10:7, 8). Jesus didn't overstate things when He promised, " 'Destroy this temple, and I will raise it again in three days' " (John 2:19). The reason people came to Christ with their calamities is they suspected what Jesus knew—God can. God can deal with all our needs—even the fear of death.

God has conquered death. Imagine facing a scenario in which you needed a specific type of surgery and you had two doctors to choose from. One surgeon really wants a chance to do the surgery, and the other doctor has successfully performed several surgeries just like the one you need.

---

* Cited in Craig Brian Larson, *750 Engaging Illustrations,* 108, 109.

Whom do you choose? Dr. Ambitious or Dr. Experienced? One wants to; the other has.

When you realize that God has already proven Himself to be able to overcome death, it inspires confidence. Consider the other individuals—other than Lazarus—resurrected from the dead who lived to tell about it.

The widow of Zarapheth's son:

> Some time later the son of the woman who owned the house became ill. He grew worse and worse, and finally stopped breathing. . . .
>
> . . . Then he [Elijah] stretched himself out on the boy three times and cried to the LORD, "O LORD my God, let this boy's life return to him!"
>
> The LORD heard Elijah's cry, and the boy's life returned to him, and he lived. Elijah picked up the child and carried him down from the room into the house. He gave him to his mother and said, "Look, your son is alive!" (1 Kings 17:17–23).

The Shunamite woman's son:

> The child grew, and one day he went out to his father, who was with the reapers. "My head! My head!" he said to his father.
>
> His father told a servant, "Carry him to his mother." After the servant had lifted him up and carried him to his mother, the boy sat on her lap until noon, and then he died. . . .
>
> When Elisha reached the house, there was the boy lying dead on his couch. He went in, shut the door on the two of them and prayed to the LORD. Then he got on the bed and lay upon the boy, mouth to mouth, eyes to eyes, hands to hands. As he stretched himself out upon him, the boy's body grew warm. Elisha turned away and walked back and forth in the room and then got on the bed and stretched out upon him once more. The boy sneezed seven times and opened his eyes (2 Kings 4:18–35).

The unnamed man tossed into Elisha's tomb:

> Elisha died and was buried.
>
> Now Moabite raiders used to enter the country every spring. Once while some Israelites were burying a man, suddenly they saw a band of raiders; so they threw the man's body into Elisha's tomb. When the body touched Elisha's bones, the man came to life and stood up on his feet (2 Kings 13:20, 21).

Jairus's daughter:

> All the people were wailing and mourning for her. "Stop wailing," Jesus said. "She is not dead but asleep."
>
> They laughed at him, knowing that she was dead. But he took her by the hand and said, "My child, get up!" Her spirit returned, and at once she stood up. Then Jesus told them to give her something to eat (Luke 8:52–55).

The widow of Nain's only son:

> As he approached the town gate, a dead person was being carried out—the only son of his mother, and she was a widow. And a large crowd from the town was with her. When the Lord saw her, his heart went out to her and he said, "Don't cry."
>
> Then he went up and touched the coffin, and those carrying it stood still. He said, "Young man, I say to you, get up!" The dead man sat up and began to talk, and Jesus gave him back to his mother (Luke 7:12–15).

Dorcas—the compassionate servant:

> In Joppa there was a disciple named Tabitha (which, when translated, is Dorcas), who was always doing good and helping the poor. About that time she became sick and died, and her body was washed and placed in an upstairs room. . . .

Peter sent them all out of the room; then he got down on his knees and prayed. Turning toward the dead woman, he said, "Tabitha, get up." She opened her eyes, and seeing Peter she sat up. He took her by the hand and helped her to her feet. Then he called the believers and the widows and presented her to them alive (Acts 9:36–41).

Eutychus—the sleepy young man:

Seated in a window was a young man named Eutychus, who was sinking into a deep sleep as Paul talked on and on. When he was sound asleep, he fell to the ground from the third story and was picked up dead. Paul went down, threw himself on the young man and put his arms around him. "Don't be alarmed," he said. "He's alive!" (Acts 20:9, 10).

God has already set a precedent of victory over death, giving everyone who believes an undeniable anchor point to grasp. The fact God can—and that God has—beat death positions every believer to trust that God will raise the dead on the resurrection day.

God will conquer death. When time is up and history has run its course, the top item on God's priority list is to remove death from reality. It is as if the score is 100 to 0 and there are ten seconds on the clock. The crowd is cheering, and everyone is waiting for the buzzer to ring. Victory is certain, but not a present reality. So God counts down the seconds and, when the buzzer sounds, He can roar, " 'Where, O death, is your victory? / Where, O death, is your sting?' " (1 Corinthians 15:55).

The Bible is rich with passionate anticipation of the resurrection. Paul leans forward with eyes sparkling as he conveys the greatest notion the human heart will ever conceive:

Listen, I tell you a mystery: We will not all sleep, but we will all be changed—in a flash, in the twinkling of an eye, at the last trumpet. For the trumpet will sound, the dead will be raised imperishable, and we will be changed (1 Corinthians 15:51, 52).

Eternal life is a promise. It's real. It is what God desires most of all. Listen to the words of Christ and how badly He wants to kick death in the teeth and end this mess, bringing everyone home:

> "This is the will of him who sent me, that I shall lose none of all that he has given me, but raise them up at the last day. For my Father's will is that everyone who looks to the Son and believes in him shall have eternal life, and I will raise him up at the last day" (John 6:39, 40).

God can, God has, and God will raise up those who chose to believe. Paul sums it up well: "By his power God raised the Lord from the dead, and he will raise us also" (1 Corinthians 6:14).

Walking through a park, I passed a massive oak tree. A vine had grown up along its trunk. The vine started small—nothing to bother about. But over the years the vine had gotten taller and taller. By the time I passed, the entire lower half of the tree was covered by the vine's creepers. The mass of tiny feelers was so thick that the tree looked as though it had innumerable birds' nests in it.

Now the tree was in danger. This huge, solid oak was quite literally being taken over; the life was being squeezed from it. But the gardeners in that park had seen the danger. They had taken a saw and severed the trunk of the vine—one neat cut across the middle. The tangled mass of the vine's branches still clung to the oak, but the vine was now dead. That would gradually become plain as weeks passed and the creepers began to die and fall away from the tree.

How easy it is for the fear of death to maintain a strangling grip on our lives. But now, Christ has cut away the power of death. Even though the vines may cling to us, they are dead and will fall away.

The question is, " 'Do you believe this?' " (John 11:26).

" 'Yes, Lord,' she [Martha] told him, 'I believe that you are the Christ, the Son of God, who was to come into the world' " (verse 27).

That's a good answer.

Questions for Reflection and Study

1. Have you lost in death someone you love very much? Has that experience strengthened your faith in God or weakened it?

2. Are you more a "Martha" or a "Mary"—more a person of action or a person of reflection? What do you see as the negatives and positives of each type?

3. Can we believe and not believe at the same time? What light does Mark 9:23, 24 shed on the relationship between faith and doubt—certainty and uncertainty?

4. In what way is Jesus' resurrection a guarantee that death is not the final end for those who accept Him?

5. What do you think Jesus meant by saying, "I am the resurrection and the life"? What does that mean for us, the living, who are facing death, and for those who have died?

CHAPTER 13

The Law of Expectation

"Do you want to be whole?"

Some time later, Jesus went up to Jerusalem for a feast of the Jews. Now there is in Jerusalem near the Sheep Gate a pool, which in Aramaic is called Bethesda and which is surrounded by five covered colonnades. Here a great number of disabled people used to lie—the blind, the lame, the paralyzed. One who was there had been an invalid for thirty-eight years. When Jesus saw him lying there and learned that he had been in this condition for a long time, he asked him, "Do you want to get well?"

"Sir," the invalid replied, "I have no one to help me into the pool when the water is stirred. While I am trying to get in, someone else goes down ahead of me."

Then Jesus said to him, "Get up! Pick up your mat and walk." At once the man was cured; he picked up his mat and walked.

—John 5:1–9

*   *   *   *   *

William Temple, archbishop of Canterbury, wrote, "We block Christ's advance in our lives by failure of expectation." Some have said, "If you don't expect much, you will never be disappointed."

I used to view big days like birthdays and Christmas from that perspective, but looking back now, I see that I couldn't squelch the longing and the hope of a big day. I would tell myself, "Relax, you are going to get just a sweater," but deep inside I suspected more was possible. I fought the urge to entertain the notion of a new bike or a football. No matter how much you tell yourself to expect less, you still want more.

The subject of this chapter is about the unnamed man Jesus questioned by the pool of Bethesda. Perhaps the most disturbing part of this encounter is how the lame man's expectations were like his legs—paralyzed. But Jesus arrived to tenderly teach him the law of expectation.

Various studies report that the law of expectation is real. Jerry Bamburg's research "clearly establishes that teacher expectations do play a significant role in determining how well and how much students learn."* Students often "rise or fall to the level of expectation of their teachers. . . . When teachers believe in students, students believe in themselves. When those you respect think you can, you think you can."†

Conversely, if teachers perceive students lack ability or the will to learn concepts or skills, students tend to mirror such expectations. How unfortunate that some students who come from particular social, ethnic, or economic settings can sense that their teachers view them as "incapable of handling demanding work."§

Bruce Wilkinson, the author of *The Seven Laws of the Learner* and *The Prayer of Jabez* tells a story about his first year of teaching. After he graduated from seminary, he took a teaching role at Multnomah School of the Bible and taught a freshman class titled "Bible Study Methods." On registration day, he was assigned sections one, two, and three. A seasoned professor pointed out to Bruce that section two consisted of a special honors class.

"Every year," Bruce said, "the students with the highest scores were placed in that class." This particular tenured teacher did not fail to men-

---

* Jerry Bamburg, *Raising Expectations to Improve Student Learning* (Oak Brook, Ill.: North Central Regional Educational Laboratory, 1994).

† James Raffini, *Winners Without Losers: Structures and Strategies for Increasing Student Motivation to Learn* (Needham Heights, Mass.: Allyn and Bacon, 1993).

§ Peggy Odell Gonder, *Caught in the Middle: How to Unleash the Potential of Average Students* (Arlington, Va.: American Association of School Administrators, 1991).

tion his surprise that a first-year teacher was so honored to be called on to teach section two.

On the first day of class, the session went well, but when section two came in, the difference was noticeable as he started to teach. Believing fully that the capacity for learning was greater, he sensed that the tone of the classroom seemed to follow his expectations. The students were thoughtful, they engaged in the discussion, and their questions were insightful. Perhaps this was not so much so with the other sections. The academic dean asked about what he enjoyed most about his first year of teaching, and Bruce answered, "Section two."

"Why section two?" the dean inquired.

Bruce replied, "Because they are the honor students, the students with the highest scores. The cream of the crop."

The dean looked confused. He said slowly, "Section two is not an honors class anymore. We stopped separating the honors students into a single class a couple of years ago."

Bruce felt a weight in his stomach, and his hands began to sweat because, if this were true, nothing the students learned in his class could match the lesson this new teacher just learned. He sought out the registrar and asked for the list of all the honors students in his classes. The registrar informed him, "All the sections have about the same number of honor students."

The weight in Bruce's stomach grew heavier as he poured over the grade book and discovered that the section two grades were noticeably better than those of sections one and three. He even took the test booklets containing the final essay exams, stacked sections one and three together, and placed them next to section two and pressed them down to see who had produced the most. Section two stood taller than sections one and three combined.

Bruce Wilkinson learned an unforgettable lesson about the law of expectation—expectations have a lot to do with outcomes.

So Jesus came to the pool of Bethesda (which means "mercy"), reputed to be a deep spring possessing supernatural properties when the water moved. Even today, similar shrines exist. Lourdes, in southern France, boasts of a spring that many believe possesses healing capacities. Also, the shrine of Guadalupe, in Mexico City, is a place thousands have ventured to in hope of healing. Whether anyone is healed or not, people come believing.

It was a common feature of the ancient world to show reverence for water. The Baganda tribe, in what is now called Uganda, believed that the Nile River was alive and, if someone fell in, they should not thwart nature by trying to save them. Barclay notes, "Hesiod, the Greek poet, said that when a man was about to ford a river, he should pray and wash his hands, for he who wades through a stream with unwashed hands incurs the wrath of the gods."*

In fact, the Bible tells of many great wonders that occurred in the context of water: the Red Sea parting; Naaman being healed of leprosy, dipping seven times in the dirty river; water coming from a rock; and so forth.

I'm not so cynical that I can't believe it's possible to have a small pond that restored people back to health. After all, some men threw a dead guy on the bones of Elisha in a tomb, and the dead man came to life like popcorn on a hot griddle. My point is that *anything* is possible. But in this case, belief in the healing powers of the pool was probably more of a fable—what we call an urban legend. Ellen White describes the scene in these words:

> At certain seasons the waters of this pool were agitated, and it was commonly believed that this was the result of supernatural power, and that whoever first after the troubling of the pool stepped into the waters, would be healed of whatever disease he had. Hundreds of sufferers visited the place; but so great was the crowd when the water was troubled that they rushed forward, trampling underfoot men, women, and children, weaker than themselves. Many could not get near the pool. Many who had succeeded in reaching it died upon its brink. Shelters had been erected about the place; that the sick might be protected from the heat by day and the chilliness of the night. There were some who spent the

---

* William Barclay, *The Gospel of John*, 178.

night in these porches, creeping to the edge of the pool day after day, in the vain hope of relief.*

Even if the pool were magical, it would have been nearly impossible for this man to qualify for a dip because of his infirmity. It's like the young person who is trying to get some work experience but the employer needs someone with experience. The man by the pool reminds us of the seven-year-old at the ball park, sitting there with his leather mitt, hoping to catch a home-run ball, though he is barely four feet tall. Amid the overzealous sports fans, he has a better chance by looking needy and having someone give him a ball than he has at squeezing the leather and snagging a homer himself.

Barclay adds insight into what might have been this man's mental state. "The man had waited for thirty-eight years and it might well have been that hope had died and left behind a passive and dull despair."

Do you know someone who has reached the point where hope is dead?

Stephen Covey's *Seven Habits of Highly Effective People* asserts that the first habit has to do with being proactive. Being proactive means asserting conscious control over your life, setting goals, and working to achieve them. Conversely, reactive people are slaves to their circumstances and deem themselves incapable of achievement. The man at the pool seems to have operated from a reactionary point of view. Can you blame him? Thirty-eight years without victory is too high a mountain to climb, especially alone. Perhaps this was why Jesus, although firm, recognized this man's desperation and asked a penetrating question that truly speaks to the heart of all of us: " 'Do you want to get well?' " (John 5:6).

I don't know one person who wouldn't be touched in some way by that question. Who doesn't have something in his or her life that is broken, empty, or unfinished? No one is completely full, whole, and in no need of help. And those who pretend to have no need are often the most broken and empty of all.

---

* *The Desire of Ages*, 201.

Even as Jesus asked the question, the lame man broke forth in a diatribe of excuses that completely did away with proactive thinking. I have observed people less patient than Jesus give up too soon on those who have given up on themselves.

The day before Thanksgiving a few students and I gathered up several boxes full of food for a family in need. The students were alive with a deep sense of meaning and purpose in taking time to help a local family. But their sentiment of purpose got sucked out of the air when the man who received the boxes roared, "Where's the ham?"

I explained that we hadn't brought a ham, but there were other items, such as turkey, which we hoped would make their Thanksgiving nice. He wanted ham. We left the food with the family and climbed back into the van, where the students expressed their disappointment, candidly. "That was the most ungrateful thing to say," echoed around the van. But Veronica said calmly, "Wait a second; I'll be right back."

She jumped out. Another friend joined her, and before I could object they were ringing the doorbell. This time an elderly woman answered and pulled them inside. I was supposed to be the group's leader, so I got out and went to try to smooth out the whole situation. The belligerent man was watching TV, while the girls cheerfully spoke with a kind woman who pulled us onto the porch and explained, "I'm so sorry about Billy's behavior. He's not well. I was in the back room doing laundry when you came. I'm so grateful for the food, and Billy will be as well. He loves food."

The girls had gone to offer to help cook the food and encountered the kind woman instead. Veronica and her friend would not be easily thwarted and had decided to give help another try.

Christ would not be thwarted by the paralyzed man's reactionary thinking. " 'I have no one to help me into the pool,' " he whined (John 5:7). Instead of rebuking him for not recognizing the greatest Helper in the world, Jesus simply commanded him, " 'Get up! Pick up your mat and walk' " (verse 8).

There are only two elements that Christ needs from us in order to start us on a journey to wholeness—the desire to be whole and the will to cooperate with Him.

The desire for wholeness is connected to our expectations. When someone desires to be well, he expects something better. Even though the desire may be weak, it is enough for Christ to strengthen and expand into a stronger, more fervent expectation. Notice the way the Savior compelled a desire for healing in this situation:

> The sick man was lying on his mat, and occasionally lifting his head to gaze at the pool, when a tender, compassionate face bent over him, and the words, "Wilt thou be made whole?" arrested his attention. Hope came to his heart. He felt that in some way he was to have help.*

If we have an inherent urge to change, then transformation is possible. When I lived in Michigan, I met Vicki, a woman who requested help to quit smoking. "I've tried so many times before; I don't know why I should try again, but I'm here," she admitted, somewhat passively.

Having observed the difficulty family members and friends had had to break this addiction, I grew suspicious, wondering, *Does Vicki have the desire?*

One day she called me and exclaimed, "Get over here right now!"

I drove by her house to see how she was doing; she was pacing back and forth in her front yard, yelling, "I don't want to do this anymore!"

After a few minutes she calmed down, and I asked, "Vicki, do you want to quit?"

"I want to quit quitting!" she stated with a scowl.

So, I asked another question: "Well, which do you want more—to quit or to quit quitting?"

Vicki had reached a point of desperation in the process of removing the nicotine from her system. I felt a lot of sympathy for her because while she seemed a bit passive at first, the fact she was wrestling so viciously with the habit now revealed her desire.

"I want to quit smoking," she told me—adding a few other words not suitable for recording in this book, but you get the message. If

---

* *The Desire of Ages*, 202.

there is desire, there is an expectation, and expectation is, really, hope.

Jesus perceived that the lame man had the desire, which is the starting point to wholeness. But in addition to desire, the human soul must exercise the will. "The power of God never dispenses with the effort of man. Nothing is truer than that we must realize our own helplessness; but in a very real sense it is true that miracles happen when our will and God's power co-operate to make them possible."*

The Bible says, "At once the man was cured; he picked up his mat and walked" (John 5:9). So, how much effort did the lame man contribute? Was it 50 percent? Or more like 5 percent? Trying to quantify the will is as impossible as counting the shape of the color yellow. You get my point.

Cooperate. One definition is "to work together to accomplish a common aim." A secondary meaning is "to do what you are asked to do." Both definitions fit needs of the moment for the man at the pool of Bethesda. We don't know if he felt sensation in his legs, which caused him to try to stand, or if he simply obeyed the words of Christ and got up. But does it really matter which came first? Jesus asked a penetrating question: "Do you want to be well?" The man did, but he didn't know how to bring that about. Nevertheless, Jesus urged him to get up and carry the mat that had been used to carry him.

Do you want to be whole? What part of your life is paralyzed today? Perhaps you face a decision in your life that requires a leap of faith, and you are scared. It probably seems easier to remain unchanged and, in a way, it is easier, but it is not better. Or maybe you need to break free from an addiction that is destroying your soul, your joy, even your home. Jesus knows you want to—or you wouldn't be reading this book.

Are you willing to stand? It is an undeniable reality that you will not overcome alone. You need to cooperate with God and others who have taken their stand. Jesus made His purpose on earth clear to us: " 'For judgment I have come into this world, so that the blind will see' " (John 9:39). " 'I have come that they may have life, and have it to the full' " (John 10:10). " 'I have come into the world as a light, so that no one who be-

---

* William Barclay, *The Gospel of John*, 180.

lieves in me should stay in darkness' " (John 12:46). " 'I came into the world, to testify to the truth' " (John 18:37). " 'For the Son of Man came to seek and to save what was lost' " (Luke 19:10).

Questions for Reflection and Study

1. Do you know someone who has reached the point where hope is dead?

2. What part of your life is paralyzed today?

3. When facing a significant decision that requires change, is it sometimes better to simply remain as you are or to move forward in spite of the pain involved? Defend your answer.

4. What part do expectations play in what actually happens? How important is willpower in bringing about change in our lives? How important is faith in bringing about change in our lives?

5. What is the one thing you would change about your life if you had the choice? What specific steps could you take today to begin making that change a reality?

CHAPTER 14

Preaching What You Practice

"Do you understand what I have done for you?"

When he had finished washing their feet, he put on his clothes and returned to his place. "Do you understand what I have done for you?" he asked them. "You call me 'Teacher' and 'Lord,' and rightly so, for that is what I am. Now that I, your Lord and Teacher, have washed your feet, you also should wash one another's feet. I have set you an example that you should do as I have done for you. I tell you the truth, no servant is greater than his master, nor is a messenger greater than the one who sent him. Now that you know these things, you will be blessed if you do them."

— John 13:12–17

*   *   *   *   *

It's 3:52 P.M., and, as I write, two Chevy Suburbans, loaded with high-school and college students, pull up, and the kids swarm my front yard with rakes. Bryson Bechtel. Chris Terry. Alan Newbold. Joel Willard. Grant Gustavsen. Justin Wampler. Ardoynx Day. Jerod Anderson. Greg McKelvey. Adam Newbold. Robert Hogan. Their fevered intensity is inspiring, especially compared to my obvious lackluster approach of putting off the yard work for weeks.

They just launched out into the neighborhoods looking to serve. They clearly were having a lot of fun. I suspect they might have been thinking, *What we are doing is a good thing, but it doesn't necessarily change the world.* But they helped more than they thought. When your life is pressed on every side, you let things slide (your health, your friendships, the yard work); and everyday things, such as leaves, pile up, littering your life with a continual reminder of what you don't do.

I'll never be able to muster the energy they exerted on those defenseless semidried leaves. At first I felt awkward and wondered, *Why don't they go help someone who really needs help?* But in truth, I did need their help. I know half of them well, and they are men of good character. And although they might be great guys as individuals—they are even mightier as a crowd.

It's 4:18 P.M. now, and they just departed. Twenty-six minutes of their combined service saved me about six hours of work that I never would have gotten around to doing. Thanks, guys!

After washing His disciple's feet, Jesus asked, " 'Do you understand what I have done for you?' " (John 13:12). Have you ever been asked a question to which you thought you had the right answer—or at least that you understood some of the answer—but you struggled to respond because there might be something further you had missed? When my teachers would explain a math problem or diagram a sentence, they would often ask, "Do you understand?" If you said No, that would be embarrassing but not as humiliating as saying Yes and then being asked to demonstrate your knowledge (or lack thereof). What were the disciples supposed to say to the question "Do you understand what I have done for you?"

When Peter initially refused to have his feet washed, Jesus said, " 'You do not realize now what I am doing, but later you will understand' " (verse 7). So, to a certain degree, the lesson Jesus sought to teach was a work in progress; but at the end, He popped the question, "Are you guys getting this?"

Nobody, even Peter, wanted to say a word. So, Jesus unpacked the question's answer for them. " 'You call me "Teacher" and "Lord," and rightly so, for that is what I am. Now that I, your Lord and Teacher, have washed your feet, you also should wash one another's feet. I have set you an example that you should do as I have done for you. I tell you the truth, no servant is greater than his master, nor is a messenger greater than the one who sent him. Now that you know these things, you will be blessed if you do them' " (verses 13–17).

Several facets of servanthood emerge from this event in the upper room—facts that may help you answer the question.

When Jesus began washing His disciples' feet, He did something no one would expect or easily accept. First of all, a rabbi simply didn't do the work of a common servant. The teacher was a wise man and a guide, not a foot washer. Second, any rabbi that would stoop to such a lowly place would not be living up to the honor of the title. And yet, time and again Jesus broke the mold and gave a new picture of God.

The disciples would have gladly washed their Master's feet, but Jesus did not issue that command; He called them to an even more difficult task—to serve one another. Anyone could wash Jesus' feet, but could a disciple wash *anyone's* feet? That was the question. The heart of a servant is revealed in the attitude with which he serves others. Anyone can do service, but not everyone has a servant's heart.

A friend pointed out to me a simple, yet profound, concept about service. There are activities many participate in, but for different reasons. A Buddhist might engage in the same activity as a Christian, but do so from a completely different motivation. You don't have to have the attitude of a servant to be of service. Some serve others out of duty or guilt or to be able to gain the upper hand. In order to grow a servant's heart, you need the right reference point, and no view is clearer than the scene at the upper room. Jesus Christ strips away any sense of self-absorbed pretense and bathes the feet of His followers. Robert Greenleaf has built a monumental system of leadership based upon the story of the Savior who washes your feet. The focus is first and foremost about others.

You may have heard the well-known story of four chaplains who served during World War II—George Fox, a Methodist minister, who had already served as a soldier during World War I; Rabbi Alexander Goode, who wrote a book some twelve years prior to World War II, forecasting the rise of Nazi Germany; Clark Poling, a Dutch Reformed minister whose letters left behind a legacy of faith and courage; and John Washington, a Catholic priest who used to be a member of a street gang. Why do we remember these four men?

In 1943, these men served in the army as chaplains and were heading to Nazi-occupied Europe on a ship named the *Dorchester*. During the voyage, the chaplains encouraged and inspired those on board, providing comfort to men suffering from seasickness and, more important, from the anxiety of war. On February 3, 1943, a German submarine torpedoed the *Dorchester*. The ship began to sink quickly into the icy waters.

The four chaplains guided and instructed the men throughout the mad scramble to deploy the lifeboats. When the supply of life vests ran out, the four chaplains removed their own and gave them to the soldiers, knowing it meant they themselves would certainly perish. The four men were standing arm-in-arm at the top of the boat singing hymns as the ship disappeared beneath the waves.

These four men personify Paul's challenge to the Philippian church to mirror the mind of Christ:

> Do nothing out of selfish ambition or vain conceit, but in humility consider others better than yourselves. Each of you should look not only to your own interests, but also to the interests of others. Your attitude should be the same as that of Christ Jesus: Who, being in very nature God, did not consider equality with God something to be grasped, but made himself nothing, taking the very nature of a servant, being made in human likeness. And being found in appearance as a man, he humbled himself and became obedient to death—even death on a cross! (Philippians 2:3–8).

Such is the distinction between service and the heart of a servant. The heart is where the service begins; the service is how the heart grows to be more like Christ. So, let's look at service, the work of a servant.

Jesus taught by example, not just in the upper room but throughout His life. Practice what you preach or maybe even better, preach about what you have been practicing. As I wander through the New Testament, the life of the Christian church is peppered with examples of works of service: "Command them to do good, to be rich in good deeds, and to be generous and willing to share" (1 Timothy 6:18). "Live such good lives among the pagans that, though they accuse you of doing wrong, they may see your good deeds and glorify God on the day he visits us" (1 Peter 2:12). "Serve one another in love" (Galatians 5:13). " 'In the same way, let your light shine before men, that they may see your good deeds and praise your Father in heaven' " (Matthew 5:16). " ' "I was hungry and you gave me something to eat, I was thirsty and you gave me something to drink, I was a stranger and you invited me in, I needed clothes and you clothed me, I was sick and you looked after me, I was in prison and you came to visit me. . . .

" ' ". . . I tell you the truth, whatever you did for one of the least of these brothers of mine, you did for me" ' " (Matthew 25:35–40).

The overarching principle is that working on behalf of others is essential to a relationship with God. Service is the classroom where we learn to live on earth as we will live in heaven.

A classic preach-after-you-practice moment came to me during an unexpected visit to a classroom.

I was visiting my wife while she worked on developing a remedial program for students. I found myself spending lunchtime in the first grade. I enjoyed watching the students rustle around the classroom with their lunch pails and small boxes of milk. I noticed one boy with bright-red curly hair who remained in his seat. My heart sank into my stomach as someone announced out loud what was obvious to anyone watching, "Billy doesn't have a lunch."

At first, I thought the remark was cruel. But before I could react, the room full of students scurried into action. What I saw seared the most beautiful image of community into my mind. Each student began breaking off pieces of their peanut-butter and jelly sandwiches and placed them on a tray that was being passed around the room. I never saw who started the tray. Bags of chips popped open and littered the brown plastic cafeteria tray with samples of every flavor known to first-graders. A half of a banana, tons of carrots and celery, and a bounty of cookies broken in half joined the rest of the items. As the tray filled with food was set before the hungry boy, a grin crept shyly across his sweet freckled face. Embarrassed? A little. Tickled to death at the feast fit for five first-graders looming before him like a small mountain? No question. Actually, I had many questions. Who started the tray? When did they learn to do this? Why hadn't *I* forgotten *my* lunch?

I asked the teacher, "Where did they learn to do that?"

He smiled. "It happened a few years back when one of my students would share his lunch with anyone who forgot theirs. Everyone joined in, and then it just became kind of an unspoken rule in the classroom. When someone forgets a lunch, everyone helps." I was stunned by the simple way the kids created community in their classroom.

Two aspects of service were vividly portrayed by that class. First, when everyone gives, what is given is so abundant that it leaves those who are helped with an unmistakable sense of God's abundant grace. And second, the service was started when one child noticed and called the others to action. The work of service has the power to deepen and stretch the life of a servant into someone who resembles Christ more fully. Whenever I ask young adults to describe a time in their lives when they felt closest to God, they usually cite seasons of tragedy or loss when they learned to lean on God and to depend upon Him for support. They also mention equally, if not more, that they felt close to God as they were serving others.

Jesus said, " 'Now that you know these things, you will be blessed if you do them' " (John 13:17). How do we learn to be a servant?

Knowing and doing are two different parts of the equation. No one realized more clearly than Jesus that it's possible for someone to know and still not do. Jesus concluded the Sermon on the Mount with the parable of the two foundations:

> "Everyone who *hears* these words of mine and *puts them into practice* is like a wise man who built his house on the rock. The rain came down, the streams rose, and the winds blew and beat against that house; yet it did not fall, because it had its foundation on the rock. But everyone who *hears* these words of mine and *does not put them into practice* is like a foolish man who built his house on sand. The rain came down, the streams rose, and the winds blew and beat against that house, and it fell with a great crash."
>
> When Jesus had finished saying these things, the crowds were amazed at his teaching, because he taught as one who had authority, and not as their teachers of the law (Matthew 7:24–29, emphasis supplied).

Hearing and doing—these two activities do not oppose each other but cooperate. With every experience of sharing yourself on behalf of someone else, you increase your capacity to love and help others.

One question that has bothered me about service is the *Why*. Why is service so real and powerful, so life changing? I believe that when we serve others with a selfless heart, we become, if only for a moment, the person God created us to be. God is selfless, and this is what I adore about Him. He is also holy and powerful, but what brings me to my knees in worship is that He set aside everything to come down to earth and die for me. That kind of selflessness sticks to you. And when we kneel down and wash someone else's feet through humble service, we become a little like God.

Acts of service to others may not seem to have a universal impact. But as you cooperate with Christ, He expands the impact in ways you may never understand. When those students came and raked the leaves in my yard, I thought of a story told about Ignace Paderewski, one of Poland's famous concert pianists and prime minister.

A devoted mother brought her young boy to one of Paderewski's concerts, hoping to encourage the young lad's progress. She purchased seats in the front row of the auditorium in an effort to inspire the young boy. She turned for a moment to speak with someone, and when she looked back her son was nowhere to be found. It was time for the concert to start when she discovered where her son had gone. Her son sat down at the piano on stage and began to pluck "Twinkle, Twinkle Little Star." She gasped and got up to remove her son, but just then the famous pianist entered the spotlight and moved to the side of the boy and whispered, "Keep playing." His left arm circled around the boy and began adding the bass part, and soon he reached out his right arm to add a running obbligato. The master musician and the young novice mesmerized the crowd with perhaps the most glorious arrangement of "Twinkle, Twinkle Little Star" ever heard.

I suppose that our acts of service are a lot like the little boy on the piano. We do our best, and God fills in around us making something more beautiful than we imagined our efforts would ever produce.

When Jesus asks the question, "Do you understand what I have done for you?" the answer should not be "Yes, I get it; I'll get started on that tomorrow." That would be incorrect. If you really want to answer that question, you begin your answer by your action. Whether your heart longs to bring help to the broken or you simply know it is the right thing to do—do it. Your active answer is part of a more elaborate scheme to get you to walk in the shoes you were born to walk in. Paul reminds us that "we are God's workmanship, created in Christ Jesus to do good works, which God prepared in advance for us to do" (Ephesians 2:10). In fact, the work of the church just might well be summed up by the author of Hebrews who urges, "Let us consider how we may spur one another on toward love and good deeds" (Hebrews 10:24).

Questions for Reflection and Study

1. In Jesus' day, washing someone's feet was a menial task that symbolized humility. What task might Jesus have used to get across the same point if He were living on earth today? What would you find most distasteful—and difficult—to do for another?

2. Explain in your own words what you think this statement means: "Anyone can do service, but not everyone has a servant's heart." What does it mean to have a "servant's heart"?

3. Does serving others always require humility? What other motives might one have for serving others? Make a list of "good" motives and "bad" motives. Is there a common thread that runs through each list?

4. In what ways does serving others benefit the one who serves?

5. What does Jesus' act of washing the disciples' feet tell us about Him? About God the Father?

CHAPTER 15

The Only Viable Option

"Do you want to go too?"

On hearing it, many of his disciples said, "This is a hard teaching. Who can accept it?"
Aware that his disciples were grumbling about this, Jesus said to them, "Does this offend you? What if you see the Son of Man ascend to where he was before! The Spirit gives life; the flesh counts for nothing. The words I have spoken to you are spirit and they are life. Yet there are some of you who do not believe." For Jesus had known from the beginning which of them did not believe and who would betray him. He went on to say, "This is why I told you that no one can come to me unless the Father has enabled him."
From this time many of his disciples turned back and no longer followed him.
"You do not want to leave too, do you?" Jesus asked the Twelve.
Simon Peter answered him, "Lord, to whom shall we go? You have the words of eternal life. We believe and know that you are the Holy One of God."
Then Jesus replied, "Have I not chosen you, the Twelve? Yet one of you is a devil!" (He meant Judas, the son of Simon Iscariot, who, though one of the Twelve, was later to betray him.)

— John 6:60–71

* * * * *

There is a story about two New Yorkers who had never been out of the city. They decided that they had had it with city living, so they bought a ranch down in Texas in order to live off the land like their ancestors.

144

The first thing they decided they needed was a mule. So, they went to a neighboring rancher and asked him if he had a mule to sell. The rancher answered, "No, I'm afraid not."

They were disappointed, but as they visited with the rancher for a few moments, one of them saw some honeydew melons stacked against the barn and asked, "What are those?"

The rancher, seeing they were hopeless city slickers, decided to have some fun. "Oh," he answered, "those are mule eggs. You take one of those eggs home and wait for it to hatch, and you'll have a mule." The city slickers were overjoyed at this, so they bought one of the melons and headed down the bumpy country road toward their ranch. Suddenly they hit an especially treacherous bump, and the honeydew melon bounced out of the back of the pickup truck, hit the road, and burst open. Seeing in his rearview mirror what had happened, the driver turned his truck around and drove back to see if he could retrieve his mule egg.

Meanwhile a big old Texas jackrabbit came hopping by and saw this honeydew melon burst in the road. He hopped over to it, and standing in the middle of that mess, he began to eat. Here came the two city slickers. They spied their mule egg burst open and this long-eared creature in the middle of it. One of the men shouted, "Our mule has hatched! Let's get our mule."

But seeing those two men coming toward it, the jackrabbit took off, hopping in every direction with the two city slickers in hot pursuit. The two men from New York gave everything they had to catch him, but finally they could go no farther. Both men fell wearily on the ground gasping for air while the jackrabbit hopped off into the distance. Rising up on his elbow, one of the men said to the other, "Well, I guess we lost our mule."

The other man nodded grimly. "Yes, but you know," he said, "I'm not sure I want to plow that fast anyway."*

Fair-weather ranchers! Where is their sense of commitment?

---

* James S. Hewett, *Illustrations Unlimited* (Carol Stream, Ill.: Tyndale House Publishers, 1988), 98, 99.

A similar question could be asked of the broad spectrum of disciples who lingered around Jesus throughout His ministry. Early in Jesus' ministry, the crowds were large, following Jesus, cramming into homes, and making it difficult for Him to move from one place to the next. But there came a point when what Jesus was saying became too hard to hear and what He was doing too hard to stomach.

Instead of bringing down Rome, Jesus spoke of going to His certain death at the hands of the people. In this particular scene Jesus refers to Himself as, "the 'living bread that came down from heaven' " and says that " 'if anyone eats of this bread he will live forever' " (John 6:51, 54). He went on to talk about drinking His blood (see verses 53–55). Worse yet, He said all this in the synagogue where officials, spiritual leaders, and perhaps a few kids were present. The saints did not receive the message well. In fact, "From this time many of his disciples turned back and no longer followed him" (verse 66). But the Twelve stood there, a pivotal moment thrust upon them by Jesus. Perhaps there was an awkward silence in which everyone was thinking, *Did He just say that?* No one dared say a word—not even Peter.

It was at such a moment that Jesus created a crossroads for the twelve disciples. He opened the back door in case anyone wanted to exit. He didn't want to lose anyone, as evidenced by the nature of His question, "You don't want to leave too, do you?" The question almost has a pitiful quality to it, doesn't it?

But how does that question come to you today? Have you ever thought of giving up and walking away from Christ? Perhaps the response the disciples gave will also give you something to think about, but even more, something to believe with a deep and abiding determination.

Peter did, at last, speak up on behalf of the disciples and conveyed their decision to stay with Christ. But notice that their answer had four parts, and so should ours as we commit to our enduring journey with Christ.

1. Deduction: "Lord, to whom shall we go?" There is a science to writing multiple-choice questions. Believe it or not, some people in the academic world argue over whether a multiple-choice question should take the form of an incomplete statement or the form of a question. Some discuss whether multiple-choice questions should be used at all if the correct answer is not objectively right or wrong. My favorite is the suggestion that multiple choice questions should offer answers that are "plausible distracters." That's right; they've made a technical name for what we all know to be the "trick question." One thing is sure: for Peter and the disciples, there are no "plausible distracters." In fact, Peter offers a question, "Lord, to whom shall we go?"

My paraphrase might go like this: "Hello, Jesus! Where are we going to go from here? We have seen way too much. In spite of all the things that might be freaking us out right now, following You is still the only real option."

The disciples left their nets, their families, their tax booths, and their security because they became convinced that the kingdom of God had arrived. Even though there were a few things to sort out—such as, "What in the world did He mean by 'eat His flesh and drink His blood'?"—each day with Jesus they became more sure that He was the Christ.

Don't take too long thinking about this question. Many are coming to the point in their lives that they feel something is missing.

In an interview in *Rolling Stone* magazine, Brad Pitt muses about the current state of things in Hollywood:

> I know all these things are supposed to be important to us, the car, the condo, our version of success . . . but there is still this feeling out there reflecting more impotence and isolation and desperation and loneliness. If you ask me, I say forget all this, we have got to find something else. Because all I know is that we are heading for a dead end, a numbing of the soul. A complete atrophy of spiritual being. And I don't want that.*

"So, what should we do?" the interviewer asked.

> Hey man, I don't have those answers yet. The emphasis now is on personal gain and success, and I'm sitting right in the middle

---

* *Rolling Stone*, October 28, 1999.

of it, and I'm telling you, "That's not it." I'm the guy that has got everything, and once you have got everything, you are left with yourself.*

There is a void in the human experience that only Christ can fill, and the disciples are keenly aware of this. So, have you done the math, made your deductions, or even scanned some of the options available for those who suspect there might be something other than God? There is value in looking at the information beforehand, so you can make an informed decision. But information alone has never filled the heart or satisfied the human soul. The basic truth is that people are hungry for what Christ offers.

Craig Dykstra observes, "The thousands of self-help groups that now flourish throughout our country are filling a vacuum created by the loss of practicing communities of devotion."[†]

To the question, "Do you want to go too?" the disciples answer, "Where else is there to go?"

Philip Yancey, when considering the meaning of this exchange admits,

> That, for me, is the bottom-line answer to why I stick around. To my shame, I admit that one of the strongest reasons I stay in the fold is the lack of good alternatives, many of which I have tried. Lord, to whom shall I go? The only thing more difficult than having a relationship with an invisible God is having no such relationship.[§]

It's not glamorous, but it is honest, and simple deduction sometimes may be the best place to start answering such a pivotal question. What would be most unfortunate is to walk away from Christ without giving it much thought at all.

---

* Ibid.

† Craig Dykstra, *Growing In the Life of Faith* (Louisville, Ky.: Geneva Press, 1999), 8.

§ Philip Yancey, *Reaching for the Invisible God* (Grand Rapids, Mich.: Zondervan, 2002), 38.

2. Fact: "You have the words of eternal life." Not only do the disciples declare that following Jesus is their only viable option, they claim, " 'You have the words of eternal life' " (John 6:68).

There is no mistaking the life-altering impact of Christ's teaching. Jesus taught with such refreshing clarity and profound insight that even the children were drawn to Him. The words He spoke were not always new. In fact, in some cases, they were quite familiar. But Jesus breathed new meaning into them. Especially in the Sermon on the Mount, Jesus fleshed out what the old text said but did so with vivid color and surprising relevance.

The inspiration for writing this book connects back to a visit I made to the country of Malawi in Africa. I sat under a mango tree with almost forty people gathered for a simple Bible study. I noticed a young man flipping through some pages of text—just pages, no cover. After everyone dispersed, I asked the young man, "I noticed you have several pages of paper, may I ask what they are?" His eyes grew wide with fear, but I assured him, through a translator, that I meant no harm. As the translator negotiated the conversation back and forth, I discovered the papers were pages from the four Gospels containing the words of Christ in red. Evidently a group of gospel workers had traveled through his village and left a Bible. He and his friends had worn this Bible to the point that it was falling apart. After several tapings, the pages would not stay together so they divided up the Bible between them, and he chose the four books full of the words of Christ.

Jesus said about His own words, " 'Heaven and earth will pass away, but my words will never pass away' " (Matthew 24:35). " 'If anyone is ashamed of me and my words in this adulterous and sinful generation, the Son of Man will be ashamed of him when he comes in his Father's glory with the holy angels' " (Mark 8:38). " 'There is a judge for the one who rejects me and does not accept my words; that very word which I spoke will condemn him at the last day' " (John 12:48). " 'If you remain in me and my words remain in you, ask whatever you wish, and it will be given you' " (John 15:7).

Christ's words were rich in content, capturing the beauty of a Creator as well as being potent enough to still the storm and cast out the demons of hell. His words conveyed the matchless love of the Father with tender simplicity; they also divided the hypocrite from the genuine seeker. One reason the disciples could not walk away was because they had seen too much, and now they had heard too much to leave.

3. Conviction: "We believe." John Stott once claimed, "If to believe in Jesus was man's first duty, not to believe in him was his chief sin." Very few words carry as much meaning as the word *believe.* Imagine if I were to come home from jogging and point to a chair saying, "I believe that chair will give me rest. I believe that it is comfortable. I believe that it is sturdy." But the only thing that would truly demonstrate my "belief" is if I were to sit in the chair. In fact, the word *believe* in our contemporary world is far too theoretical compared to the biblical meaning. In the Bible, to believe is not simply to accept something as true but to depend upon it for your life. The difference is real when you do the "trust fall."

Every year, the high school senior class ventures into the woods for "senior survival." Among the activities is what is called a "trust fall," one of several group initiative games that deepens camaraderie and has tremendous power to teach the truth about what it means to believe. A student stands on top of a six-foot platform and simply falls backward into the arms of their classmates. But the "trust fall" is not always so simple because there is a crucial moment when the student truly commits. They can stand and lean back, but they don't release control until they reach the point of no return. Commitment is crucial to believing.

Some people hold "beliefs" they have not committed to. Some maintain opinions that are not tested or internalized. When the disciples announced to Christ, "We believe," they had crossed from the world of simple ideas to the land of faith. John Stuart Mill observed, "One person with a belief is equal to a force of ninety-nine who have only interests."

Are you a believer? Have you leaned past the tipping point in regard to your commitment to Christ?

4. Determination: "We believe and know that you are the Holy One of God." According to Reuters news agency, Alberto Gauna, of Argentina, became so depressed that he decided to end his own life. He placed the .22 caliber pistol to his right temple and pulled the trigger. The gun fired but, much to his surprise, he was still alive. Determined to finish the job, he pointed the pistol at his forehead and fired, but that did not kill him either. After a third and fourth shot to his head, he shot himself in the stomach, but his body still refused to die. By the time he stopped shooting himself, he had fired six shots into his own body but still lived. What is more amazing—his determination to die or his determination to live?*

The disciples extend the level of their commitment to Christ, adding, " 'We believe and know that you are the Holy One of God' " (John 6:69). The disciples had not only an active belief, they had the earnest determination of those who "know" they are right. And we all know people who know they are right.

I knew I was right in staying on the freeway for one more exit when my wife tried to tell me to exit right away. As I blew by the exit, I even ruminated on the heavy responsibility one bears when he is as knowledgeable as I am. Then came the bridge and the long trek to the other side of the river, which included a long, humiliating drive back. My determination did not play out the way it did for the disciples, who stood next to Christ when the crowds were leaving. Their faithfulness was mixed with moments of shortcomings and distractions, but these men answered Christ's question with deliberate confidence.

I wish I could answer this question for you as Peter did for the other disciples. And there are days when I would rather have you answer for me because I just don't have the courage.

But the disciples—despite being criticized for their faults—are true believers in Christ and determined followers of the Savior. Answering this question may bring you to a crossroads of sort, or it may simply be a no-brainer to say to Jesus, "I'm not going anywhere, except to follow You." Either way, say it yourself, because your strength renews itself, and the doors open when you answer the questions God asks.

---

* Reuters, "Man Shoots Self Four Times in Head But Lives," *America Online,* November 1, 1994, http://www.aol.com.

Questions for Reflection and Study

1. Have you ever thought of giving up and walking away from Christ? If so, what kept you from doing so?

2. Is it possible for a person to hold to beliefs that he or she is not committed to? What is the difference between believing and committing?

3. If there is a void in the human experience that only Christ can fill, why do the great majority of persons on earth live their lives without reference to Him—without following Him or believing in Him?

4. This chapter speaks of a "tipping point" in terms of our commitment to Christ. What would be a "tipping point" for you—the point beyond which nothing could shake your confidence in Jesus as your Savior? Do you feel there is such a point for you? Is there a "tipping point" in the other directions—a point that pushes you to abandon Him?

5. List the top five reasons—in order of importance to you—why you follow Jesus.

CHAPTER 16

Full Disclosure, Full Restoration

"Do you love Me?"

When they had finished eating, Jesus said to Simon Peter, "Simon son of John, do you truly love me more than these?"

"Yes, Lord," he said, "you know that I love you."

Jesus said, "Feed my lambs."

Again Jesus said, "Simon son of John, do you truly love me?"

He answered, "Yes, Lord, you know that I love you."

Jesus said, "Take care of my sheep."

The third time he said to him, "Simon son of John, do you love me?"

Peter was hurt because Jesus asked him the third time, "Do you love me?" He said, "Lord, you know all things; you know that I love you."

Jesus said, "Feed my sheep."

— John 21:15–17

* * * * *

There is a maxim in the angler community, told from the viewpoint of a fisherman's wife. It says, "Give a man a fish, and he eats for a day. Teach a man to fish, and you get rid of him for the whole weekend."

Jesus' question in this chapter takes place in the context of a fishing expedition. Apparently, on that day everyone went fishing. It started with Peter, but nobody was leaving Peter alone, so the whole band of disciples climbed on board. But their night of fishing was unsuccessful.

Both of my brothers are serious fishermen. My dad taught them right, but I didn't learn a thing. I hate fishing. I don't like losing, and every time I fish, I can see the fish avoiding my bait. On one fishing trip in the mountains, the trout in the lake seemed to mock me openly. Frustrated by the constant waiting and waiting, and being still and being quiet and waiting, I almost went nuts. Finally, I lost it when I watched a rainbow trout staring at my bait for sixteen minutes. I began launching rocks at the fish in a tirade of frustration. Of course, all the other fishermen stared at me in disgust. I hate fishing because I hate waiting, and I hate losing.

I understand the lack of success Peter and the others endured, but a voice came across the water shouting, " 'Friends, haven't you any fish?' " (John 21:5). This is not *the* question for this chapter, but paraphrased it reads, "Hey, ya young whippersnappers—had any luck?" The cagey old fishermen would always ask me that question, too, and I would often want to reply, "If I had any luck I'd be at the doughnut shop instead of staring into the water waiting for some slimy, smelly creature to get deceived and chew on the accoutrements fastened to the end of my line." But instead I would answer, "Nope."

The disciples answered, "No," and Jesus urged them to throw their net on the right side of the boat. He promised, " 'You will find some' " (verse 6). They obeyed the Master, and the fish obeyed Him. The entire scene smacked of the good old days, and now they knew what they had suspected all along: Jesus had come to visit them. Peter dove in, and they convened at a lakeside campfire where Jesus had been cooking fish. Ellen White comments on the dejá vu of the scene:

> Vividly they recalled the scene beside the sea when Jesus had bidden them follow Him. They remembered how, at His command, they had launched out into the deep, and had let down their net, and the catch had been so abundant as to fill the net, even to breaking. Then Jesus had called them to leave their fishing boats, and had promised to make them fishers of men. It was to bring this scene to their minds, and to deepen its impression, that He had again performed the miracle. His act was a renewal of the commission to the disciples. It showed them that the death of

their Master had not lessened their obligation to do the work He had assigned them.*

But during this little encounter Jesus pulled Peter aside and asked him a few questions that are well-known. But have they been well-answered?

It is possible that Peter didn't want to answer any questions or enter the spotlight. Not just because of his recent betrayal but also in light of his eloquent promise to die with Jesus, if it came to that. To falter and fail exposed Peter's weakness as a human, but to promise unparalleled loyalty just prior to caving in was simply shameful. Even though hope had returned to the gang of believers, you have to wonder what Peter was thinking. If nothing else, it took the edge off of his bravado. When you begin to doubt yourself, you're careful with your commitments and your words.

The questions Jesus asked Peter could be symbolic or rhythmic. Peter denied Christ three times, so it was only appropriate to restore Peter with a three-step consecration. But I wonder if the real reason Jesus asked three times was that Peter was guarded and didn't quite trust himself. Perhaps Jesus was drawing him out. Either way, Jesus' ultimate goal was full disclosure because Peter wouldn't be able to fulfill his role as an apostle if he weren't confident in his leadership. I think Jesus knew that Peter wouldn't fully give his life for the cause if he didn't experience full disclosure and full pardon. Jesus was Peter's Teacher, and He would coach him through this slump.

"When they had finished eating, Jesus said to Simon Peter, 'Simon son of John, do you truly love me more than these?' 'Yes, Lord,' he said, 'you know that I love you.' Jesus said, 'Feed my lambs' " (John 21:15).

What did Jesus mean by "more than these"? Recall the night of Peter's betrayal. Peter had promised, " 'Even if all fall away on account of you, I never will' " (Matthew 26:33). Peter was always making comparisons. For example, "Peter came to Jesus and asked, 'Lord, how many times shall I forgive my brother when he sins against me? Up to seven times?' " (Matthew 18:21). Of course, the Pharisees taught that you had to forgive your

---

* *The Desire of Ages*, 810, 811.

enemy only three times, but Peter thrusts out his spiritual chest and raises the bar.

If Peter hadn't broken his promise to Christ, he might have answered, "Are You kidding? There isn't another soul within a hundred miles who loves You more than I do!" But this time Peter didn't overstep nor overstate. In fact, he invited Jesus to interpret his simple answer. " 'Yes, Lord,' " he said, " 'you know that I love you' " (John 21:15).

When Jesus charged Peter to "feed my lambs," He was tenderly, respectfully, inviting him to rejoin the team. The Lord was entrusting to Peter the cause of the kingdom. His language was affectionate and respectful. Nothing would empower Peter more than for someone to openly believe in him.

The second question Jesus asked Peter was: " 'Simon son of John, do you truly love me?' " (verse 16). The Greek word Jesus used here is a form of *agape*—an unconditional benevolence toward another person, regardless of who they are or what they do. This kind of love is typical of God but rare with His children. It's interesting that although Jesus used this word, Peter responded using a different Greek word—a form of *phileo*, which refers to the affectionate love for a friend or a loved one. Perhaps Peter had learned a valuable lesson—to promise less and deliver more.

> Before his fall, Peter was always speaking unadvisedly, from the impulse of the moment. He was always ready to correct others, and to express his mind, before he had a clear comprehension of himself or of what he had to say. But the converted Peter was very different. He retained his former fervor, but the grace of Christ regulated his zeal. He was no longer impetuous, self-confident, and self-exalted, but calm, self-possessed, and teachable.*

Working through a problematic season with a married couple taught me about promising less and delivering more. The husband had good intentions, even the noblest aspirations, for the family and his relationship with his wife, but he would never follow through. During one session, the

---

* *The Desire of Ages,* 812, 815.

wife put her foot down and said, "I don't believe you. You have never kept your promise, and I won't do this anymore!"

He got the message but never said a word. Instead, little by little, he began to deliver.

Let's look at Jesus' last question to Peter—question number three: " 'Simon son of John, do you love me?' " (verse 17). The Bible says that "Peter was hurt because Jesus asked him the third time" (verse 17). Perhaps Peter distrusted himself so much that the third question seemed as though Jesus didn't believe in him.

There have been times when I suspect my son hasn't been entirely truthful with me, that I ask him the same question over and over in order to give him a subtle chance to come clean. Is that what Jesus was doing here? In His third question, instead of using the *agape* word, Jesus uses the *phileo* word—the same word Peter had just used in replying to His second question. This implies that Jesus knew where Peter stood and that He was going to accept him now, right where he was. Jesus might be saying, "Peter, right now you are giving Me all you have, and that is all I need from you. Get to work, My friend."

To Jesus' final question, Peter simply pleads, " 'Lord, you know all things; you know that I love you' " (verse 17). Clearly, he just wanted Jesus to hear his heart and read his mind because he didn't trust his mouth. But it was still a worthwhile exercise to say the words, "You know that I love you."

Imagine the Savior asking you this simple question today: "Do you love Me?" What do you say? It's quite all right to say what you truly think: "I do love You, Lord, but look into my heart and see for Yourself." What this answer implies is "I know I love You, but I also know that I should love You more, and I want to." Peter made a comeback. Henry Ford said, "Failure is the opportunity to begin again more intelligently."

In 1879 a child was born into the family of a poor Jewish merchant. He grew up in a community that voiced strong anti-Semitic sentiments that made him feel self-conscious and fearful. He was so shy, and his behavior so slow, that his parents had him examined to see if he were mentally handicapped. When he grew older, he tried to get accepted into a university in Zurich but failed the entrance examination. He tried again the next year and passed. Although he earned a doctorate, he could find work only as a patent examiner. Never discouraged by his circumstances or his own failures, Albert Einstein ultimately succeeded. Now his name is used synonymously with *intelligence.*

Just as Einstein became the poster boy for brainiacs, Peter became a pivotal leader in the early stages of the new church. In Acts 2, Peter stood up and preached to thousands of people, calling them to receive Jesus as the Messiah of the Old Testament promises, and three thousand were baptized. In Acts 3, Peter and John walked through the temple gate where a crippled man begged for help. Peter's response was, " 'Silver or gold I do not have, but what I have I give you. In the name of Jesus Christ of Nazareth, walk' " (Acts 3:6). Peter was clear about his identity and role. In connection with his healing of the beggar, Peter was arrested, questioned, and released, but through all of it, he pointed to the Savior and gave Him all the glory and praise. Peter's life spoke volumes. In his life and his death, Peter communicated his enduring love for Jesus.

After speaking at a conference, I was talking with some friends about this story, and someone asked, "How do you know when you love God?" At first the answer seemed so obvious, "You just know." But that didn't seem to satisfy the group.

How do you know when you love God? When you long for contact with Him. "O God, you are my God, earnestly I seek you; my soul thirsts for you, my body longs for you, in a dry and weary land where there is no water" (Psalm 63:1).

When Jesus initially called the disciples, "He appointed twelve—designating them apostles—that they might be with him" (Mark 3:14). Do you find you are drawn to Christ, not only by a feeling but sometimes by a need? How many times have you thought, *I need to get closer to God?* It doesn't matter if the thought comes from a sense of duty (like Martha) or from an internal desire (like Mary). What matters is that whatever compels you to be close to Christ comes from God. God will woo you through whatever avenue of your soul is available.

If you find yourself driven away from Him by your guilt or fear of exposure, you need to know God is not the source of that obstacle.

If you possess these qualities in increasing measure, they will keep you from being ineffective and unproductive in your knowledge of our Lord Jesus Christ. But if anyone does not have them, he is nearsighted and blind, and has forgotten that he has been cleansed from his past sins (2 Peter 1:8, 9).

The promise of God's Word is, "as far as the east is from the west, / so far has he removed our transgressions from us" (Psalm 103:12). Please don't let guilt, fear, or doubt get in the way of your intimacy with Christ. Those roadblocks are the tools of the accuser, not the work of your Creator.

We need to nurture a love-hate relationship—love God and hate evil. David urges, "Let those who love the LORD hate evil, / for he guards the lives of his faithful ones / and delivers them from the hand of the wicked" (Psalm 97:10).

I hate drinking. I think dulling your sensibilities, at any level, to any degree, is wrong. My mom and dad are amazing people of courage and integrity. When they learned of a greater way to live, they turned their back on drinking and embraced the good life with God. They love God and have no taste in their mouths for the other way. And though I have parents, I have never met my father-in-law. He was killed instantly when five drunken teenagers plowed head-on into his vehicle, almost killing Julia, his four-year-old daughter, who later became my wife.

I hate it when people prey on children and lie about it with pathological dexterity.

I hate the fact that loneliness is a real epidemic, more common than rain in Seattle.

Those who love God keep His commandments. " 'Whoever has my commands and obeys them, he is the one who loves me' " (John 14:21). If God's law is the transcript of His character, a portrayal of who He is, then I love the law, not because of what it says but because of who it portrays. John writes, "This is love for God: to obey his commands. And his commands are not burdensome" (1 John 5:3).

Some will be perplexed by this verse because it seems to contradict basic teachings about grace. But from an experiential standpoint, is it really all that hard to piece together? We know from life that rules define our relationships, perhaps not in a decalogue or a list but certainly in spirit.

If Peter's story by the shore teaches us anything, it's that even when we fall, we don't fail unless we resist the restoration Christ extends. Peter knew not to spurn grace and became an expert in the field of overcoming. Peter's final words recorded in Scripture were, "Grow in the grace and knowledge of our Lord and Savior Jesus Christ" (2 Peter 3:18). In a way, Peter offers a simple but profound truth—the only way to truly grow through failure is to grow through grace.

Questions for Reflection and Study

1. What effect do you think Peter's denial of Jesus just before the Crucifixion had on his willingness to stand up boldly for Jesus following the Resurrection? Did Peter have something to "prove"?

2. Have you ever experienced something similar to Peter's devastating denial of Jesus? If so, how did you deal with it? What effect has it had on your subsequent relationship with Jesus?

3. How do you "know" when you love God? What role does obedience play in love?

4. What does Peter's story tell us about Jesus' willingness to restore those who have fallen and who repent? What does Jesus require of us before He will restore us to His fellowship?

5. How can we use failure in the process of growth?

CHAPTER 17

Just Your Average, Normal Prophet

"Who will go for Us?"

In the year that King Uzziah died, I saw the Lord seated on a throne, high and exalted, and the train of his robe filled the temple. Above him were seraphs, each with six wings: With two wings they covered their faces, with two they covered their feet, and with two they were flying. And they were calling to one another:

"Holy, holy, holy is the LORD Almighty; the whole earth is full of his glory."

At the sound of their voices the doorposts and thresholds shook and the temple was filled with smoke. "Woe to me!" I cried. "I am ruined! For I am a man of unclean lips, and I live among a people of unclean lips, and my eyes have seen the King, the LORD Almighty."

Then one of the seraphs flew to me with a live coal in his hand, which he had taken with tongs from the altar. With it he touched my mouth and said, "See, this has touched your lips; your guilt is taken away and your sin atoned for."

Then I heard the voice of the Lord saying, "Whom shall I send? And who will go for us?"

And I said, "Here am I. Send me!"

— Isaiah 6:1–8

* * * * *

Have you ever sold someone the wrong ice-cream cake? Few people can make such a claim, but I can.

Working at Baskin-Robbins was a joyful experience—for the most part. But I also found that dealing with difficult ice-cream customers can sometimes be off the charts. Ice-cream people are serious about their ice cream, and there is no dissatisfied customer like the one who arrives at the store intending to bring home a custom ice-cream cake—only to find out that it has been sold to someone else.

"A round cake made with mint chocolate-chip ice cream sandwiched between a layer of fudge and chocolate icing." The moment she asked for the cake, a deep sinking feeling dropped into my stomach like a bowling ball. I had just sold what I thought to be the only mint chip cake to someone else thirty minutes ago. There were three of us working that night, and we all knew what was coming, so we met in the back to talk about strategy.

"What do we do?" I asked.

"We?" cried the other two. "*You* sold her cake!"

Bolstered by an internal surge of lionlike courage, I begged, "Would you please talk to her for me?" (The lion I was referring to was a costar on *The Wizard of Oz*—that lion.)

I listened behind the backroom door as Jill went out to "deal with the customer."

"I'm so sorry, Tro—I mean, we—don't have your cake, but I can make you one in a few minutes."

"What do you mean? I ordered the cake this morning!" she shouted (as I said earlier, people are passionate about their ice cream).

"I'm so sorry," Jill said again, as she cut more ice cream and spoke kindly to the irate lady. "We think we might have accidentally sold the cake to someone earlier, accidentally that is."

She said all this while looking at the back door, vigorously urging us to come out and help. We continued to hide.

"Well, who did you sell my cake to?" the customer demanded.

She wants to know the identity of the person who now has her cake? This is bad. What is she going to do—track her down and yank the cake from the innocent recipient's freezer?

Jill just looked at her with a blank stare that conveyed one emotion: despair. Other customers were waiting. People were murmuring. Things looked hopeless.

Isaiah, too, knew hopelessness. In this case, God's questions arose when Heaven came to visit Isaiah in a vision concerning the nation of Judah.

The young prophet was frustrated by the way Israel was spiraling blindly toward destruction. Luxury and vice were stealing the starch out of the spiritual life of the nation, and Isaiah's messages were falling on deaf ears. Ellen White comments on the sad state of affairs during the time when Isaiah was a prophet:

> The outlook was particularly discouraging as regards the social conditions of the people. In their desire for gain, men were adding house to house and field to field. . . . Justice was perverted, and no pity was shown the poor. Of these evils God declared, "The spoil of the poor is in your houses." "Ye beat My people to pieces, and grind the faces of the poor." . . . Even the magistrates, whose duty it was to protect the helpless, turned a deaf ear to the cries of the poor and needy, the widows and the fatherless. . . .
>
> With oppression and wealth came pride and love of display, gross drunkenness, and a spirit of revelry. . . . And in Isaiah's day idolatry itself no longer provoked surprise. . . . Iniquitous practices had become so prevalent among all classes that the few who remained true to God were often tempted to lose heart and to give way to discouragement and despair. It seemed as if God's purpose for Israel were about to fail and that the rebellious nation was to suffer a fate similar to that of Sodom and Gomorrah.*

When your job as a prophet is to openly confront this kind of problem, how do you get out of bed and go to work? Whenever I have students who come in and complain, saying, "My situation is hopeless; I'm depressed," I often use Isaiah as my own mental measuring rule to assess depression. Although I don't—and won't—ever do this, I'm sometimes tempted to say, "You think you're depressed? Your life is a birthday party compared to Isaiah's." Everyone has drama and challenges that seem insurmountable, which is why—instead of comparing and accosting each other—we should

---

* Ellen G. White, *Prophets and Kings* (Mountain View, Calif.: Pacific Press® Publishing Association, 1943), 306.

seek to understand each other and to identify what it is like when the task ahead of us seems hopeless.

Isaiah understood depression. Ellen White adds, "He well knew that he would encounter obstinate resistance. As he realized his own inability to meet the situation and thought of the stubbornness and unbelief of the people for whom he was to labor, his task seemed hopeless."*

At the darkest hour God ushered Isaiah in to His throne room and gave the prophet a vision of glory. But instead of giving Isaiah a set of marching orders that would surely overwhelm him, God gave him an abundance of grace that enabled the humble prophet to stand.

> "Woe to me!" I cried. "I am ruined! For I am a man of unclean lips, and I live among a people of unclean lips, and my eyes have seen the King, the LORD Almighty."
>
> Then one of the seraphs flew to me with a live coal in his hand, which he had taken with tongs from the altar. With it he touched my mouth and said, "See, this has touched your lips; your guilt is taken away and your sin atoned for" (Isaiah 6:5–7).

The same is true for you and me whenever we face our darkest hour or an impossible challenge with humility. God pours out amazing grace on us.

Alex Haley, the author of *Roots,* had a picture hanging on the wall of his office. It was of a turtle sitting on top of a fence. When people asked about the picture, he explained, "When you see a turtle sitting on top of a fence, you know that he had help getting there." Throughout history, the great men and women of faith stand as a memorial of God's grace. But we know it is because they had help getting there. A classic example of this is Isaiah the prophet.

After Isaiah was "purified," God asked the prophet a question. " 'Whom shall I send? And who will go for us?' " (Isaiah 6:8). It's pretty obvious, isn't it? Isaiah has been prepared for this calling. Bathed in the mercy of heaven, Isaiah stood before the God who asks questions. The angels were

---

* Ibid., 307.

watching. It was for Isaiah to answer, and he responded, " 'Here am I, send me!' " (verse 8).

Key to the question God asked is "Who?"

Well, the knee-jerk answer to that question would be, "A prophet."

The Hebrew word for prophet is *nabi,* which means "one who is called by God." Throughout history the prophets have held a fundamental role in God's interactions with people. The writer of Hebrews explains:

> In the past God spoke to our forefathers through the prophets at many times and in various ways, but in these last days he has spoken to us by his Son, whom he appointed heir of all things, and through whom he made the universe (Hebrews 1: 1, 2).

There have always been men and women who call people back to God and draw their attention to His Word. And the people God chooses are pretty normal.

For as long as I can remember, I have always had a dog. It's kind of weird the way people give their dogs outlandish names. Just think of some of the dogs you know. Does the name their owners give them really match their characteristics? My neighbor has this little Chihuahua. He named the tiny creature "Bruiser." Maybe the dog was so fragile that he bruised easily. Or maybe this pup is a real sleeper—a dog that looks wimpy but has the power to do some real damage. Another friend named his enormous St. Bernard "Zacchaeus." You can tell a lot about the owner of a dog by the name he gives his pet. Consider "Tiggy," for example—a beautiful, fun-loving, somewhat-mischievous dog that was named after a great Assyrian leader—Tiglath-Pileser III. It's possible that there were similarities between the leader and the dog, but how weird is it that someone would name a dog after a mighty Assyrian leader? It does seem kind of weird, but on the other hand, maybe not so much. You see, Tiggy was Ellen White's treasured pet, a normal dog with a normal dog name given by someone who was pretty normal. It's true. Ellen White was a prophet who had a dog named Tiglath-Pileser III!

I think one of the qualities about famous people that we forget over time is how normal they were. A president who had a bad knee. Poets who were tone deaf and couldn't carry a tune in a bucket. Generals who easily got the hiccups. World-changers who were so afraid of heights they would freak if they had to climb up three rungs on a ladder.

In ancient times prophets were considered important people, but the truth is—they were just people. More often than not, prophets were wanted dead or alive because they spent most of their time warning God's people of danger. Often, the message was a rebuke or a passionate plea to wake up. The messages of the prophets were often hard to hear but necessary. Noah, Moses, Elijah, Daniel, and Isaiah had some wild things to say *for God*. That's what made them special. Prophets don't just speak *about* God; they often speak *for* God. Who wants that job?

I was going to take a bunch of young people up the mountain to go skiing. We had been planning this event for months, and the kids were excited. It was snowing, and the snowfall was just pouring down. Then I received a phone call from a parent who was already up the mountain, saying the road was icy and the authorities were telling travelers not to come up. The forty-six students on the bus were oblivious to this as I talked on the phone.

I couldn't risk their lives just because they so desperately wanted to ski. I knew that. I also knew that telling them was going to be painful. They were going to riot. Their disappointment would be directed at me, not because they hated me but because of the message I would bring. They would be angry. They would question my decision. They would undermine my knowledge of weather and roads. They would make excuses. Blame the church for not supporting its young people. Call me "stupid" under their breath—but they would live to see another snow day.

I told the bus driver to turn around and made the announcement. As I expected, the crowd focused their disappointment on the person who gave the message. I sat down in my seat, alone except for the bus driver (who I think was mad at me too).

As our bus rumbled slowly down the mountain, bright lights of ambulances and fire trucks roared by us in a furious dash to get up the mountain. One by one, they passed us with their lights blazing. The disgruntled mood on the bus began to change as the kids began to pray with each other for the victims. Others joined in. The warning was right. While I was not their hero, by any means, the gravity of the moment and the message got through. And though not grateful, they understood.

Prophet of God. Any seventeen-year-olds want that job? Can you imagine how hard it must have been to confront kings and leaders and angry mobs of people? What is so amazing is that these awesome messages were given by ordinary people, who may have had a dog named Tiggy or Biff or Punchy or Roscoe or Spot or Sam.

Someone has to go when God calls because someone will listen. Even though, like Elijah, you may think you are standing for God all alone, someone is listening, watching, and thinking about the message. Isaiah's task was unbelievably difficult. No one seemed to be listening. Yet, God's message in the book of Isaiah has a thematic thread that runs through it—the remnant, a group of people who remain. There were always some who listened, as these texts demonstrate:

A remnant will return, a remnant of Jacob will return to the Mighty God. Though your people, O Israel, be like the sand by the sea, only a remnant will return (Isaiah 10:21).

In that day the LORD Almighty will be a glorious crown, a beautiful wreath for the remnant of his people (Isaiah 28:5).

Once more a remnant of the house of Judah will take root below and bear fruit above (Isaiah 37:31).

Out of Jerusalem will come a remnant, and out of Mount Zion a band of survivors. The zeal of the LORD Almighty will accomplish this (Isaiah 37:32).

God's call to Isaiah is the same call He extended to the New Testament Christians. " 'You will receive power when the Holy Spirit comes on you;

and you will be my witnesses in Jerusalem, and in all Judea and Samaria, and to the ends of the earth' " (Acts 1:8).

What qualifies you? God has offered grace and mercy to you even before He called you. You are qualified because, while you are unique, you are normal in the same way that Elijah, Moses, Deborah, Isaiah, Daniel, and Ellen are normal.

So, when God asks, "Who will go for Me?" what is your answer today?

Questions for Reflection and Study

1. Do you sometimes feel that life is hopeless and that God is not in control? How do you deal with such thoughts?
2. Do you believe that God has a specific plan for your life? If so, how do you know what that plan is?
3. Do you agree that those whom God uses to accomplish extraordinary things are really quite ordinary people? Why, or why not?
4. What determines whether or not God is able to use a person? Do some people have the ability to accomplish more than others?
5. If God were looking for a prophet today, what do you think He would list on the job description? Would you apply for the job? Why, or why not?

CHAPTER 18

The Joy of Hearing Your Name

"Who are you looking for?"

Then the disciples went back to their homes, but Mary stood outside the tomb crying. As she wept, she bent over to look into the tomb and saw two angels in white, seated where Jesus' body had been, one at the head and the other at the foot.

They asked her, "Woman, why are you crying?"

"They have taken my Lord away," she said, "and I don't know where they have put him." At this, she turned around and saw Jesus standing there, but she did not realize that it was Jesus.

"Woman," he said, "why are you crying? Who is it you are looking for?"

Thinking he was the gardener, she said, "Sir, if you have carried him away, tell me where you have put him, and I will get him."

Jesus said to her, "Mary."

She turned toward him and cried out in Aramaic, "Rabboni!" (which means Teacher).

Jesus said, "Do not hold on to me, for I have not yet returned to the Father. Go instead to my brothers and tell them, 'I am returning to my Father and your Father, to my God and your God.'"

Mary Magdalene went to the disciples with the news: "I have seen the Lord!" And she told them that he had said these things to her.

— John 20:10–15

* * * * *

Do you remember that feeling you had in school when the teacher would call upon random students to read or answer a question? If you didn't want to answer or participate, you avoided looking at the teacher. You looked busy—writing feverishly or turning the pages of your textbook so as to look engaged and not really a candidate to call upon. But then, slicing through the anticipation and mindless busywork, your name is called, and you are more alert at that moment than anyone else in the room. Your name. It is unique, and when it is spoken, you hear it even against the backdrop of white noise or conversation.

"Mary Magdalene." Her name conjures up images of a lewd sinner who found the Savior but whose past trailed not too far behind. The Bible describes Mary as an important member of a support staff to the ministry of Christ:

> After this, Jesus traveled about from one town and village to another, proclaiming the good news of the kingdom of God. The Twelve were with him, and also some women who had been cured of evil spirits and diseases: Mary (called Magdalene) from whom seven demons had come out; Joanna the wife of Cuza, the manager of Herod's household; Susanna; and many others. These women were helping to support them out of their own means (Luke 8:1–3).

The added comment, "from whom seven demons had come out," speaks to Mary's hazy history. But when Christ entered her life, the old life became history, and her devotion to the Savior became a remarkable feature of the New Testament. Mary Magdalene is the personification of devotion. During the Crucifixion, Mary and the others stayed close because it was the only thing they could do. "Some women were watching from a distance. Among them were Mary Magdalene, Mary the mother of James the younger and of Joses, and Salome" (Mark 15:40). "Near the cross of Jesus stood his mother, his mother's sister, Mary the wife of Clopas, and Mary Magdalene" (John 19:25). "Mary Magdalene and Mary the mother of Joses saw where he was laid" (Mark 15:47).

Throughout the entire nightmare, they not only stood by the side of Christ, but they hovered over every detail. When we walk through the dark nights of loss, some fix their eyes on the menial but necessary tasks as a way to stay sane. These people are primarily doers; when there is nothing they can do about the tragedy, they do something, anything, to keep busy. Another aspect of this part of the grieving process is that a doer finds comfort in taking care of the details as a way to honor and respect the lost loved one.

Mary's walk with Jesus seems to have at least four features that make her one of the most inspiring disciples of all.

1. Experience. At one time Mary had been possessed by evil. In fact, when Luke introduces her, he describes her as the one "from whom seven demons had come out" (Luke 8:2). This is probably not the way she wanted to be remembered, but Mary's experience was forever marked by the demons Christ delivered her from.

2. Commitment. Mary's financial and moral support is noted in Luke 7, which describes a unique scene in which a group of women come together from different walks of life to be Christ's disciples.

3. Devotion. Especially during the difficult moments of that terrible weekend, Mary was there to help. She did more than help, she asserted herself near the tomb saying, " 'Sir, if you have carried him away, tell me where you have put him, and I will get him' " (John 20:15).

4. Sadness and Joy. Mary's grief was so severe she couldn't see the risen Christ through her tears. Twice Jesus spoke to her in plain view, but she was incapable of focusing her attention because she was lost without Jesus.

" 'Woman, why are you crying?' " Jesus asked her. Now, of all the things you would expect to see at a gravesite, someone crying is probably at the top of the list. Of all the things you just don't say to someone grieving, "Why are you crying?" has to be the most obvious. Is it so uncommon to be so distracted by sadness that God's voice goes unrecognized when He speaks to us in our grief?

Perhaps it was the tone of His voice that Mary recognized, but more likely it was the sound of the Savior's voice speaking her name, "Mary . . . " What I love about this moment is that in the blink of an eye, everything changed from hopelessness to joy. Ellen White comments:

But now in His own familiar voice Jesus said to her, "Mary."
Now she knew that it was not a stranger who was addressing her,

and turning she saw before her the living Christ. In her joy she forgot that He had been crucified. Springing toward Him, as if to embrace His feet, she said, "Rabboni."*

She forgot He had been crucified. Moments before, Christ's horrible death was all she could remember. She didn't recall even one of the three times Jesus had foretold His death. "The Son of Man must suffer many things and be rejected by the elders, chief priests and teachers of the law, and that he must be killed and after three days rise again" (Mark 8:31).

The human spirit is resilient and creative, but there is one reality in life that people fail to negotiate smoothly—death. When someone we love passes away, we are torn and changed in irreparable ways. It should be that way. People should never get good at getting over the loss of a loved one. Until Christ ultimately wipes away every tear and death is no more, death will always feel like an enemy that seems to always win. Perhaps this is why Paul wrote,

> Listen, I tell you a mystery: We will not all sleep, but we will all be changed—in a flash, in the twinkling of an eye, at the last trumpet. For the trumpet will sound, the dead will be raised imperishable, and we will be changed (1 Corinthians 15:51, 52).

Paul reminds us that the change from death to life is swift and sure, which causes us to reflect with confidence on Mary's conversation with the risen Jesus. God can turn our worst night into morning, in the twinkling of an eye.

The questions Jesus asked, "Mary, why are you crying? Who are you looking for?" didn't need to be answered. By the time Mary recognized Christ, the answer was irrelevant. We who live on earth and endure loss and the longest night can look at death through the lens of the resurrection, but still, it's so hard to make out the faint glow of the coming morning. Just knowing the morning *will* come may be enough. I have to believe that when Paul urged people to be informed about the resurrection, he was trying to help us get to the other side of that long night.

---

* *The Desire of Ages*, 790.

Brothers, we do not want you to be ignorant about those who fall asleep, or to grieve like the rest of men, who have no hope. We believe that Jesus died and rose again and so we believe that God will bring with Jesus those who have fallen asleep in him. According to the Lord's own word, we tell you that we who are still alive, who are left till the coming of the Lord, will certainly not precede those who have fallen asleep. For the Lord himself will come down from heaven, with a loud command, with the voice of the archangel and with the trumpet call of God, and the dead in Christ will rise first. After that, we who are still alive and are left will be caught up together with them in the clouds to meet the Lord in the air. And so we will be with the Lord forever. Therefore encourage each other with these words (1 Thessalonians 4:13–18).

One thing every believer can believe with as much heart as they have is that when Christ calls your name, you will know exactly who is calling you.

Like the worst of nightmares, I pumped the pedals of my bike desperately but seemed to be moving only in slow motion. Everything that could go wrong, had gone wrong the day of Little League tryouts. I was trying to get to the field on time. But my feet had grown during the off-season, and my cleats didn't fit. So I strapped on my standard issue canvas sneakers. Last year's baseball cap signaled I played in the minor league so I chose to remove any headgear that advertised overt or subliminal messages of my diminished ability. My leather baseball glove had become misplaced, so I scrounged up an old plastic mitt from my younger days of tee-ball. I was at the age that I could be placed again in the minors or go to the majors where the big boys played. Ill-equipped and frazzled, I skidded up to the ball field, handed in my registration papers, and took my place at the end of the line.

The boys in front of me were older, and I suspect quite evil. When they noticed my plastic mitt, they laughed and made jokes about it. They informed me I should get a haircut. Without a baseball cap, my long, straight seventies hair hung in my face like strands of wet spaghetti.

The nightmare had only just begun. Hearing my name called, I raced out onto the diamond to field ground balls and throw them to first base. When my sneakers weren't sliding on the sandy infield, the tiny plastic glove would slip as my sweaty hand tried to squeeze the baseball tight. Catching fly balls with spaghetti hair in my face, running the bases with flat shoes, trying to concentrate on hitting when the older boys were laughing and the mothers were sighing with sympathy—what a nightmare!

At the end of the tryouts the coaches called out the names of the players they had chosen, beginning with the major league candidates. I remember two emotions raging in my mind at the time—shame and hope. I had failed so miserably that I knew no coach in his right mind would pick me. Nevertheless, I hoped tentatively that there would be one coach there that day who wasn't in his right mind. Sure enough, the sweet, glorious sound of my name—Troy!—rang out from one coach looking straight at me! He waved me to his side as my hopeful heart surged with surprise, gratitude, and relief. No sound is sweeter than when you hear the One who chose you call your name.

Questions for Reflection and Study

1. Why do you think Jesus appeared first to Mary following His resurrection—rather than to one of the more prominent disciples such as John or Peter? Does this say anything about the way we perceive importance or rank?

2. Why do you think Mary failed to recognize Jesus until He spoke her name? Does Jesus know your name? What makes you think so—or what makes you think He doesn't?

3. What does it say about Mary that she was at Jesus' grave so early in the morning—before any of the other disciples had arrived? Do you think Jesus chose to reveal Himself first to Mary—or that she just happened to be the first one there that morning? Does this tell us anything about receiving blessings from Him?

4. Mary managed to overcome an unsavory past to become one of those who were closest to Jesus. What can we learn from her experience that will help us to overcome the issues that we are dealing with—both past and present?

5. Do you expect to hear Jesus call your name when He comes? How does that make you feel?

CHAPTER 19

The Master Teacher Makes It Real

"What is written in the law, and how do you read it?"

On one occasion an expert in the law stood up to test Jesus. "Teacher," he asked, "What must I do to inherit eternal life?"

"What is written in the Law?" he replied. "How do you read it?"

He answered: " 'Love the Lord your God with all your heart and with all your soul and with all your strength and with all your mind'; and, 'Love your neighbor as yourself.' "

"You have answered correctly," Jesus replied. "Do this and you will live."

But he wanted to justify himself, so he asked Jesus, "And who is my neighbor?"

In reply Jesus said: "A man was going down from Jerusalem to Jericho, when he fell into the hands of robbers. They stripped him of his clothes, beat him and went away, leaving him half dead. A priest happened to be going down the same road, and when he saw the man, he passed by on the other side. So too, a Levite, when he came to the place and saw him, passed by on the other side. But a Samaritan, as he traveled, came where the man was; and when he saw him, he took pity on him. He went to him and bandaged his wounds, pouring on oil and wine. Then he put the man on his own donkey, took him to an inn and took care of him. The next day he took out two silver coins and gave them to the innkeeper. 'Look after him,' he said, 'and when I return, I will reimburse you for any extra expense you may have.'

"Which of these three do you think was a neighbor to the man who fell into the hands of robbers?"

The expert in the law replied, "The one who had mercy on him."
Jesus told him, "Go and do likewise."

— *Luke 10:25–37*

* * * * *

The strangest things happen at summer camp. My conviction in this area stands, although I have no scientific evidence or statistical data to support it.

I don't know the scientific name for *a freak accident,* but one occurred at the beginning of the evening meal at summer camp one year. Junior campers packed the cafeteria and filled the hall with busy noise. I sat down at the end of a bench as eight boys pressed in together to inflict damage on their meals. The young lad sitting next to me tore into his food like a Tasmanian devil, stopping only long enough to look to see if the kitchen crew had started serving seconds. (I think Brendon was actually breathing through his ears because his mouth was preoccupied with food.)

Leaving his vegetables to the end, Brendon picked up a knife and fork to reduce the carrots to pieces of a more manageable size. His right hand gripped the knife and pressed forcefully on a stubborn carrot, but the carrot refused to be cut. He lunged even harder at it; his hands slipped, and the bottom of his forearm hit the edge of the table with an awful crack. I couldn't believe it. Neither could he. (I don't think anyone who heard the sound finished their meal.) I rushed out to get the nurse and a car to take him to the hospital. The pain increased all the way to the hospital. Strangely enough, there were two other patients getting X-rays for broken arms at the same time. (I told you the whole situation was freaky.)

The doctor brought us in as he interpreted the X-rays; the entire board was filled with pictures of the skeletons of arms. The doctor pointed to the break in the bone shown on one particular picture and said, "That's a good one, partner! Did you get bucked off a horse?" We chuckled a bit as we described Brendon's fierce encounter with the helpless carrot. As I looked at the wall, I noticed that the pictures all looked a lot the same, even though the arms belonged to a number of different people. Besides Brendon's arm, there were arms from a twelve-year-old boy, a sixteen-year-old

176

girl, and the arm of a small boy who couldn't have been more than eight. Their bones all looked pretty much the same—at least to me. Without flesh, skin, or freckles, it was difficult to determine which bones belonged to Brendon.

It occurred to me years later that skeletons need flesh to have personality. Bones need skin and color to be real. And in a way, the law is only a skeletal view of what God is like. The young lawyer's question had to do with "inheriting eternal life," and Christ redirected his query to the law of God.

The question the lawyer asked was, " 'What must I do to inherit eternal life?' " (Luke 10:25). Often, when we look at this passage, we freak out because the lawyer seems to be trying to work his way to heaven—and Jesus doesn't tell him, "Ask for mercy" or "Receive God's grace" or even, "Trust fully in the soon-to-be-finished work on Calvary." Jesus heads straight to the law. I can hear the moans coming from the "grace police." This can't be good.

However, look at the question again: " 'What must I do to *inherit* eternal life?' " It is a well-known fact that there were some in Jesus' day who felt the need to make excruciating rules to ensure their place in heaven, but this is not the case here. The lawyer isn't asking to *earn* eternal life; he's asking how to *inherit* eternal life. An inheritance is a gift granted. It's based not on deeds but on a covenant that establishes a relationship between the benefactor (that's God) and the beneficiary (that's you). Besides, the New Testament is loaded with priceless texts that convey the concept that there are things you can *do* to experience such a relationship. Consider a few:

"Blessed are the meek, for they will inherit the earth" (Matthew 5:5).

"Everyone who has left houses or brothers or sisters or father or mother or children or fields for my sake will receive a hundred times as much and will inherit eternal life" (Matthew 19:29).

We do not want you to become lazy, but to imitate those who through faith and patience inherit what has been promised (Hebrews 6:12).

Listen, my dear brothers: Has not God chosen those who are poor in the eyes of the world to be rich in faith and to inherit the kingdom he promised those who love him? (James 2:5).

Do not repay evil with evil or insult with insult, but with blessing, because to this you were called so that you may inherit a blessing (1 Peter 3:9).

"He who overcomes will inherit all this, and I will be his God and he will be my son" (Revelation 21:7).

We can dance theologically around this topic all we want, but the truth we know intuitively is, that while God has made salvation available as a gift, it comes packaged in a relationship with the Giver. That is not a hook, a cop-out, a string attached, or a legalistic loophole—it is an inescapable reality of Scripture. Theological terms are exciting to discuss and tease apart, but eventually the rubber tires of ideas must meet the road of reality, which is where the practical question emerges, "What do I do to inherit eternal life?" Another way to say it is, "How do I establish a relationship between myself and the eternal Benefactor of eternity?"

But this book is not about our questions to God as much as it is about God's questions to us. Still, Jesus answers this lawyer's question—a question that all of us should wonder about—with a series of questions of His own. Jesus is the Master Teacher.

Which teachers in your life have made the greatest impact on you and your learning? Have you ever taken time to think about what they did that was so effective? One attribute of effective teachers has little to do with what they do and more to do with who they are. Teaching is more than what you say. Parker Palmer's *Courage to Teach* is primarily about who you are as a teacher. Subrahmanyan Chandrasekhar is an example of a teacher who demonstrates how who you are affects who the student becomes:

In 1947, a professor at the University of Chicago, Dr. Chandrasekhar, was scheduled to teach an advanced seminar in astrophysics. At the time, he was living in Wisconsin, doing research at the Yerkes astronomical observatory. He planned to commute twice a week for the class, even though it would be held during the harsh winter months.

Registration for the seminar, however, fell far below expectations. Only two students signed up for the class. People expected Dr. Chandrasekhar to cancel, lest he waste his time. But for the sake of two students, he taught the class, commuting a hundred miles round trip through back country roads in the dead of winter.

His students, Chen Ning Yang and Tsung-Dao Lee, did their homework. Ten years later, in 1957, they both won the Nobel Prize for physics. So did Dr. Chandrasekhar in 1983.*

Your character and commitment are keys to effective teaching, but there are many skills and techniques teachers apply to be effective. One of those skills is asking good questions. For example, I overheard one Bible teacher ask, "What does John chapter three, verse sixteen say God did for us?" The question is mindless because the answer is effortless: "He gave His Son" the children droned with semicomatose looks in their eyes. Such a question doesn't require the student to think, feel, wonder, or apply anything. Perhaps one of the most engaging questions every teacher ought to be asking is, "What do you think?" Examine the way Jesus answered the lawyer's question with His own excellent question: " 'What is written in the Law?' he replied. 'How do you read it?' " (Luke 10:26).

The law Jesus was referring to in this conversation includes the Ten Commandments but also the first five books of the Old Testament (the Pentateuch), as well as God's revealed will through the writings of the prophets. However, we know precisely what aspect of the law Jesus and the man were referring to because the lawyer answered, " ' "Love the Lord your God with all your heart and with all your soul and with all your strength and with all your mind"; and, "Love your neighbor as yourself" ' " (verse 27). He put together a synthesis of God's revealed will, connecting the *Shema* of Deuteronomy 6:5 with Leviticus 19:18, which reads, " ' "Do

---

* Craig Brian Larson, *750 Engaging Illustrations*, 562, 563.

not seek revenge or bear a grudge against one of your people, but love your neighbor as yourself. I am the LORD." ' "

These two great themes—love for God and love for human beings—are embedded implicitly and explicitly throughout God's revealed Word. In fact, if this lawyer were an expert in the law, he would have had a small copy of the answer close by. The religious teachers in Jesus' day wore small leather boxes (called phylacteries) around their wrists containing the salient portions of the law (see Matthew 23:5). But the question wasn't "What's in your box?" Everyone knew what was written in the law. Christ asked, "How do you read it?" or "What do you think about what you have read?"

The Lord didn't appear to be dodging the issue just because this man might have been in league with those trying to trap Him. Quite the contrary. Ellen White says, "The lawyer was not satisfied with the position and works of the Pharisees. He had been studying the Scriptures with a desire to learn their real meaning. He had a vital interest in the matter, and had asked in sincerity, 'What shall I do?' "*

Jesus replied to the lawyer, " 'Do this and you will live' " (Luke 10:28). Again, the *doing* is to be done in the context of a relationship with God, not as a list of things to do or not do. When I asked a fifth-grader to paraphrase this story, she wrote about what it meant to keep the law saying, "Be a loving child of God and a good neighbor to mankind."

The practical question is, How does one *do* this? The lawyer must have thought, *Doing this requires dealing with my neighbor.* So he asked, " 'And who is my neighbor?' " (verse 29). Knowing God's will and allowing it to sink deep into our hearts are two experiences often further apart than we like to admit. As long as God's will remains theoretical, there really is no problem. Except that Jesus, as the Master Teacher, answers His pupil's question with another teaching tool—a parable.

A parable, as Michael Warden explains, "is a truth wrapped in a story. Stories make up the fabric of life. Through them we learn, we understand each other and our world, and they often lead us to change and grow."†

---

* *The Desire of Ages,* 497.

† Michael D. Warden, *Extraordinary Results From Ordinary Teachers* (Loveland, Colo.: Group Publishing, 1998), 74.

Jesus tells the lawyer the parable of the good Samaritan, perhaps the most famous parable of all. Hospitals have adopted the name to convey their mission. People, when they treat others with extraordinary kindness, are called "good Samaritans." In the mind of a Jew, there could be no more obvious oxymoron than a "*good* Samaritan." The hatred between the two groups was intense. For the Jews, there were Gentiles, and then there were Samaritans. To call someone a "Samaritan" was just about the worst insult you could hurl (see John 8:48).

Read Jesus' parable and notice how little need there is for elaborate interpretation:

> In reply Jesus said: "A man was going down from Jerusalem to Jericho, when he fell into the hands of robbers. They stripped him of his clothes, beat him and went away, leaving him half dead. A priest happened to be going down the same road, and when he saw the man, he passed by on the other side. So too, a Levite, when he came to the place and saw him, passed by on the other side. But a Samaritan, as he traveled, came where the man was; and when he saw him, he took pity on him. He went to him and bandaged his wounds, pouring on oil and wine. Then he put the man on his own donkey, took him to an inn and took care of him. The next day he took out two silver coins and gave them to the innkeeper. 'Look after him,' he said, 'and when I return, I will reimburse you for any extra expense you may have' " (Luke 10:30–35).

The story, as only a story can do, arrested the soul of the lawyer. The truth of his sinful prejudice and self-righteousness burned his conscience as Jesus fixed His gaze on him and asked, " 'Which of these three do you think was a neighbor to the man who fell into the hands of robbers?' " (verse 36). The question had an obvious answer, but the convicted man couldn't even choke out the name "Samaritan." He answered, " 'The one who had mercy on him' " (verse 37). Even more important than discovering the identity of his neighbor was his discovery of a broader, more universal principle—the concept of mercy and what it means to *be* a neighbor. Ellen White observed:

181

Thus the question, "Who is my neighbor?" is forever answered. Christ has shown that our neighbor does not mean merely one of the church or faith to which we belong. It has no reference to race, color, or class distinction. Our neighbor is every person who needs our help. Our neighbor is every soul who is wounded and bruised by the adversary. Our neighbor is everyone who is the property of God.*

The lesson learned in this parable reminds me of the words of Michael Collins, the astronaut who orbited the moon with Neil Armstrong. Asked about what he thought when he saw the earth from space for the first time, he answered,

> I think the view from 100,000 miles could be invaluable in getting people to work out joint solutions, by causing them to realize that the planet we share unites us in a way far more basic and far more important than differences in skin color or religion or economic system. That all-important border would be invisible, that noisy argument suddenly silenced. The tiny globe would continue to turn, serenely ignoring its subdivisions, presenting a unified façade that would cry out for unified understanding, for homogeneous treatment. The earth *must* become as it appears: blue and white, not capitalist or Communist; blue and white, not rich or poor; blue and white, not envious or envied. . . . There must be one earth, tiny and fragile, and one must get 100,000 miles away from it to appreciate fully one's good fortune in living on it.†

The impact of this teaching and learning moment between Jesus and the young lawyer reminds us that our eternal life is really about relationships—relationships between us and God and between us and each other.

---

* *The Desire of Ages*, 503.

† Michael Collins, *Carrying the Fire* (New York: Farrar, Strauss, and Giroux, 1974), 469–471.

It teaches us, too, that for God's law to be effective, it must be fleshed out in tangible, real ways. Otherwise, we might think right but never live right.

Finally, has it occurred to you that the work of putting religion into reality is based on your answering the question, "How do you read it?" Here is a question that, if you were to face it and answer it as honestly as did this young lawyer, could shape the way you live every day of your life.

Questions for Reflection and Study

1. Who are the "Samaritans" today—those who are looked down upon and discriminated against? What can we do as a church and as individuals to remove prejudice and animosity in our neighborhoods?

2. Which teachers have made the greatest impact on you and taught you the most? What did they do that was so effective? How can we best teach others about God's love?

3. Is there a difference between earning eternal life and inheriting eternal life? If so, what is the difference? How does that difference affect us?

4. How does the Bible define our "neighbor"? What does Jesus mean when He says that we should love our "neighbors" as ourselves?

5. What changes might take place in your life if you were to take more seriously Jesus' command to love your neighbors as yourself? What changes might take place in your relationship with Jesus?

CHAPTER 20

Almost No-Namers

"*What do you want Me to do for you?*"

Then they came to Jericho. As Jesus and his disciples, together with a large crowd, were leaving the city, a blind man, Bartimaeus (that is, the Son of Timaeus), was sitting by the roadside begging. When he heard that it was Jesus of Nazareth, he began to shout, "Jesus, Son of David, have mercy on me!"

Many rebuked him and told him to be quiet, but he shouted all the more, "Son of David, have mercy on me!"

Jesus stopped and said, "Call him."

So they called to the blind man, "Cheer up! On your feet! He's calling you." Throwing his cloak aside, he jumped to his feet and came to Jesus.

"What do you want me to do for you?" Jesus asked him.

The blind man said, "Rabbi, I want to see."

"Go," said Jesus, "your faith has healed you." Immediately he received his sight and followed Jesus along the road.

— Mark 10:46–52

* * * * *

The story of Blind Bart reminds me of something E. Paul Hovey said: "A blind man's world is bound by the limits of his touch; an ignorant man's world by the limits of his knowledge; a great man's world by the limits of his vision." The story of Bartimaeus depicts the one central desire of his heart. Prompted by a seemingly ridiculous question from

Christ, the door opens for the great Son of Timaeus.

The word *Jericho* means "to smell," which is not surprising, given the countless balsam and cypress bushes and the rose gardens that covered the region. As Jesus was leaving the city with His disciples, "a large crowd" was with them, drawing all kinds of attention to the Savior and His disciples. It was almost time for the Passover, and the Roman authorities knew that national pride would be high, which often meant insurrections. Zealots were trained assassins, seeking to take down Rome one soldier or community leader at a time. Their official name was the *Sicarri,* or "Daggermen." In fact, some suggest that Judas Iscariot, whose surname may come from the word *Sicarri,* was a son of a long line of guys skilled at using a knife. Large crowds gathering on the outskirts of cities made the Romans nervous.

There were also certain phrases that the Romans listened for and paid attention to. They knew the Jews held a religious belief that a Messiah would come and free them from their oppressors. This Messiah would be called, as the Old Testament prophecies foretold, the "Son of David." So, when some blind guy started screaming, "Jesus, Son of David!" at a large crowd of people on the outskirts of the city, the Romans were going to want to know what was going on. Romans were famous for swift, brutal responses to insurrections and for asking questions later. Perhaps this was why the disciples shushed Blind Bartimaeus when he cried out to Jesus for mercy.

As a kid, whenever I played too aggressively with my little brother and he cried, I would try to shush him, so as to avoid my parents stepping in to add some justice to my life. There were times he wouldn't shush, so I'd place my hand over his mouth, hoping suppression would quiet him down. I know!—why would I think that? His lips would somehow contort around my hand and squeal out a plea for help so desperate and so effective, that his cries only increased the measure of justice that soon came my way.

As for Bart, "Many rebuked him and told him to be quiet, but he shouted all the more, 'Son of David, have mercy on me!'" (Mark 10:48). Clearly, there were several ways to interpret Bart's response. He either was so desperate for healing that he didn't care what others said or did; he would not go unnoticed! Or perhaps not only is he blind, but he is also deaf and can't hear the rebuke or his own voice, so he desperately shouts as loud as he can. The first interpretation is more likely.

We are urged to "Love the LORD your God with all your heart" (Deuteronomy 6:5). God also promises, " 'You will seek me and find me when you seek me with all your heart' " (Jeremiah 29:13). Blind Bart sought out Christ, not with his eyes but with his heart. I'm not trying to be poetic. This blind man was not going to let anyone or anything get in his way of having a few moments with Jesus.

Notice, that when Bart cried out "all the more," Jesus stopped. Nothing arrests the attention of the Savior more than someone who wants His attention more than anything else. Jesus said to His disciples, "Call him."

All of a sudden the tone of the disciples changed. " 'Cheer up! On your feet! He's calling you' " (Mark 10:49). Bart didn't waste time saying, "I told you so," but he did do something I've never seen before. The Bible says, "Throwing his cloak aside, he jumped to his feet and came to Jesus" (verse 50). The *chiton* (cloak) was the heavy outer garment Jews wore. It was their primary garment; it kept the hot sun off of you in the daytime and you could curl up in it at night. The *chiton* had significant value; Hebrew families would sometimes give a boy a seamless linen garment when he reached adulthood. (This value is why the soldiers gambled for Jesus' cloak at the Crucifixion rather than dividing it in pieces.)

Bart "threw his cloak aside" because it was thick and cumbersome and might get in the way. Anyone who has ever had kids knows that when a child feels encumbered by clothes, you had better keep an eye on him or her because if you don't, the next thing you will see is your flesh and blood, but mostly flesh, streaking through the room or the yard naked as a jaybird. Not once have I seen a streaking child who failed to be full of glee.

Bart stripped away anything that would encumber his progress to Christ. But the blind man made one other impressive move. He jumped up. Have you ever seen a blind person jump anywhere for anything? Blindness usually causes you to be careful, and sudden movements—up, down, or side to side—are usually not healthful.

When Blind Bartimaeus finally made it to the feet of Jesus, the Lord asked him the most ridiculous question ever: " 'What do you want me to do for you?' " (verse 51).

Let's replay the tape: Here's a screaming, jumping, near-naked blind man coming right at Jesus, and the Lord asks—what? "What do you want me to do for you?"

When I hyperextended my knee, it swelled, so I wrapped it and went to see the doctor. When he came in, he quickly looked right at my wrapped knee and asked, "Did you hurt your knee?"

I wanted to say, "Nope, it's just cold. I feel great! How is your day going?" But while my mind was trained on the street, my mouth was trained by my mama, so I simply invited him to look at my knee.

What a ridiculous question!

But the question Jesus asked Bart was not a dumb question. It was an invitation. There is no circumstance in all of the Gospels in which someone gets this close to Christ and walks away dissatisfied—except Nicodemus and the rich young ruler. And their circumstances were entirely different from Bart's situation. Jesus was going to give this man whatever he asked for, but He wanted to know what Bart *really* wanted.

What do you want Jesus to do for you? It's a good question and one that requires an answer.

Bartimaeus answered, " 'Rabbi, I want to see' " (verse 51). The term *Rabbi* is not just another way to say "Teacher." It's an endearing term of commitment. In fact, in the Gospels, the only people who used that term referring to Jesus were the disciples Christ had chosen or those, like Nicodemus, who eventually came to accept him. *Rabbi* means "My Great One." You called a man *Rabbi* when you wanted to become a disciple and follow him as someone you wanted to emulate. In effect, Bartimaeus is saying, "Open my eyes so I can follow You the rest of my days."

When Jesus says, " 'Go, . . . your faith has healed you,' " Bartimaeus was healed immediately, but his true desire was filled when he "followed Jesus along the road" (verse 52). The word *road* is the same Greek word translated "way." It is no coincidence that Bartimaeus ends up on the "Way." This was the name given to early Christians.

When Saul (who became Paul) went in search of believers to persecute, he sought out people "who belonged to the Way" (Acts 9:2). Those who have refused to believe the gospel are said to have "maligned the Way" (Acts 19:9). Throughout the region "there arose a great disturbance about the Way" (Acts 19:23). Furthermore, Paul testifies in court to being "a follower of the Way"

(Acts 24:14). Even Felix, the Bible says, was "well acquainted with the Way" (Acts 24:22). The name change to "Christians" happened first in Antioch, but before that, believers in Christ were called members of "the Way."

Bartimaeus, the son of Timaeus, became a fully committed follower of Christ. Have you ever wondered why he, a blind beggar, is mentioned by name in the Bible? Mark's Gospel, scholars believe, is Peter's words written by Mark for the church in Rome. It is entirely possible that the reason the story includes the full name, Batimaeus, Son of Timaeus, is because those who read the story would recognize the name. Perhaps Bart followed Jesus on the Way and never stopped, becoming a well-known figure in the New Testament church.

Bart's story reveals several truths about our journey of life. First, Bartimaeus shows us there are some things only we individually can do to find Christ. Bart yelled, threw off obstructions, and sought Christ until he found Him. Jesus told a parable about one pearl worth everything the merchant owned (see Matthew 13:45, 46).

Second, there are some things only Christ can do for you to open the way for you to follow Him. Bart received his sight, but more important, he received the freedom to follow his ultimate desire. And finally, his story teaches us that what you do when you encounter Jesus determines the way your story is remembered. Bart and his name live on, but would he even be mentioned in Scripture if, after being healed, he simply went his own way?

In college I preached regularly in a nearby church to hone my skills as a pastor. This church held two services, and the head elder would always take the Scripture reading prior to the sermon. In the second service, this elder would, without fail, subtly critique my first sermon publicly, before reading the Scripture.

On one occasion he chided sweetly, "Our pastor has chosen Psalm one hundred thirty-nine for his sermon today. Although he will not fully capture the rich beauty of this scripture today, we should meditate on its message throughout the day."

Ouch! So I learned to temper his remarks by switching the Scripture reading for the second service to obscure passages of the Bible that required him to pronounce difficult names and places! Eventually, his sassy little diatribes ceased, and I stopped stiffing him with off-topic passages to read.

But during one particular reading at the end of Romans, something about the names that were read struck a chord of conviction in me, so I went home and thought about the unsung heroes of the faith. One truth resurfaced over and over: really, the gospel was spread by the efforts of second-generation disciples.

The names mentioned at the end of Paul's letter are not the hall-of-famers of the Christian faith. No Mary, Peter, James, or John. By the time Paul's letter to the Romans was written, Peter was probably dead, and Paul was in prison. Meanwhile, people like Bartimaeus and the list of almost no-name disciples were working tirelessly for Christ.

Here's a sample from Romans 16: "I commend to you our sister Phoebe, a servant of the church in Cenchrea. . . . She has been a great help to many people, including me" (verses 1, 2). "Greet Priscilla and Aquila. . . . They risked their lives for me. Not only I but all the churches of the Gentiles are grateful to them" (verses 3, 4). "Greet my dear friend Epenetus, who was the first convert to Christ in the province of Asia" (verse 5). "Greet Mary, who worked very hard for you" (verse 6). "Greet Andronicus and Junias. . . . They are outstanding among the apostles, and they were in Christ before I was" (verse 7).

The list goes on: Ampliatus, Urbanus, Stachys, Apelles, Aristobulus, Herodion, Narcissus, Tryphena, Tryphosa, Persis, Rufus, Asyncritus, Phlegon, Hermes, Patrobas, Hermas, Philologus, Julia, Nereus, Olympas, etc.

Tell me, when was the last time you heard a preacher preach a sermon about Tryphena and Tryphosa or Andronicus and Junias (who some scholars think was a woman)? Who ever heard of Asyncritus? (Doesn't that sound like a deadly disease or some virus you pick up slurping bad water on foreign soil?) Nevertheless, Paul painstakingly applauds these "saints" before he signs off the letter to the little church in Rome.

Some people are famous for one brave act or a brief moment of glory. Bart and the saints referred to by Paul are no "one-hit wonders"—these disciples are what I call *serial Christians*. Deliberate. Planned. Repeated. Their consistent goodness etched them into Peter and Paul's hall of fame.

Perhaps the question Jesus asked Bartimaeus is the most important question of all: "What do you want me to do for you? What is your single-minded desire?"

John Ortberg refers to research that shows how single-minded passion makes for a storied life.

> Researcher Mihaly Csikszentmihalyi did a study involving two hundred artists eighteen years after they left art school. He found that it was those who in their student days savored the sheer joy of painting that became serious painters. Those drawn to art school in hopes of wealth or fame drifted away to other professions. Painters want to paint above all else. If the artist in front of the canvas begins to wonder how much he will sell it for, or what the critics think of it, he won't be able to pursue original avenues. Creative achievements depend on single-minded immersion.*

My prayer is that our deepest desire for God will be satisfied. That we will become convicted, that the cheap wants we mindlessly seek will become worthless, and the underlying passion in our hearts for our Creator will become everything to us. That, like Bartimaeus and Chloe and Tryphena and Tryphosa, we will simply want, more than anything else, to walk in the "Way" with God. That we will want to see well enough to recognize the Way, the Truth, and the Life right in front of us. That we will want to see well enough to not fall behind or foolishly run ahead, but to walk in step with Christ.

Amen.

My son Cameron is eleven years old, and he has all the answers. There is always a response, an insight, a punchy bit of wisdom spoken with the confidence of an ancient sage from that boy. And sometimes he's even right. My other son, Morgan, is six, and he mostly has questions. His questions demand answers. It is possible that I spend most of my time with those two boys in the midst of a question or an answer. It's fun.

Questions and answers give evidence that there is contact and maybe intended communication, but only when a question is answered is there a connection. Two worlds, otherwise separate, are brought together by our response. God asks good questions that paint a picture of Him and His plan for

---

* John Ortberg, *If You Want to Walk on Water, You've Got to Get Out of the Boat* (Grand Rapids, Mich.: Zondervan, 2001), 64.

us. But His questions do more than portray Him to us—they present us with a real opportunity to draw closer to Him as our Creator, Savior, and Friend.

Some have only questions for God. The sadness and unpredictable events of life can smack the song out of anyone and leave us wanting to know what went wrong. We want explanations. There is a longing to understand because somehow we think knowing who, why, how, where, and what will make us whole. Having God answer our questions will really only create more questions. " 'As the heavens are higher than the earth, / so are my ways higher than your ways / and my thoughts than your thoughts' " (Isaiah 55:9).

What we need most are not questions for God but answers. Clearly this journey has never been about having all the information but about responding to Divine inquiry. God knows that our answers move us toward Him and with Him and even forward for Him.

Of course, there are other questions God asks people in the Bible—questions we haven't looked at in this book. Some are fairly mundane; others are priceless. But God cared about people enough to enter into our world and ask, so perhaps it is safe to say He deserves an answer. May the way you respond to God's questions bind you to Him today and bind you even closer to Him tomorrow.

Questions for Reflection and Study

1. What do you want more than anything else? Be specific. How committed are you to achieving this desire?
2. Are there some things that only we can do in order to encounter Jesus for ourselves? Can you identify what some of these might be? Make a list.
3. How do you feel when you read the names of obscure early Christians in the Bible? What does it say about the use God can make even of those who have few talents and who are not well-known?
4. In your life, what encumbrances do you need to throw off in order to come to Jesus fully? Ask Jesus to help you become aware of what you need to do and to give you the grace to do it.
5. What does the story of Blind Bartimaeus teach us about the example we can be to others and to future generations?

If you appreciated this book, you'll want to read these also:

Discovering God's Will
Troy Fitzgerald

Does God play hide-and-seek with His will? Does finding God's will for your life seem like a game show in which you must choose door A, door B, or door C? Can you choose the right door without knowing what (or who) is behind it? Is God hiding necessary information from you? Or are you hiding from God? Does using your brain have anything to do with knowing God's will?

Troy Fitzgerald, PhD, shares his conviction that you can know God's will and live happily in it. In this book you will discover principles of guidance, find scripture passages that will help you discover and do God's will even in adversity. You'll also learn the difference between devotions and true devotion to God's will.

ISBN 13: 978-0-8163-2180-3   ISBN 10: 0-8163-2180-9

Sometimes I Don't Feel Like Praying!
Mike Jones

Mike Jones knows the Seventh-day Adventist Church from the inside out. He was a popular Adventist pastor, writer, and former editor of *Insight* magazine. He was serving in the ministerial department of his conference when he went through a divorce. In response to his letter of resignation, his local church wasted no time dropping his membership. They didn't tell him. He learned about it from his son.

Mike didn't go off the deep end. He had no major differences with the church. But it would be sixteen years before he returned to the Adventist Church. This book is about grace. It will teach you how to exchange your old life for a new one. You will find tools to handle the worst that life can throw at you. How? By becoming a new you. Don't wait, start now.

ISBN 13: 978-0-8163-2229-9   ISBN 10: 0-8163-2229-5

Three ways to order:
1. Local Adventist Book Center®
2. Call 1-800-765-6955
3. Shop AdventistBookCenter.com